YEOVIL

150 Years of Railways

by

B.L. Jackson

THE OAKWOOD PRESS

© Oakwood Press & B.L. Jackson 2003

British Library Cataloguing in Publication Data
A Record for this book is available from the British Library
ISBN 0 85361 612 4

Typeset by Oakwood Graphics.
Repro by Ford Graphics, Ringwood, Hants.
Printed by Cambrian Printers, Aberystwyth, Ceredigion.

Title page: One hundred and fifty years after steam reached Yeovil, steam can still be seen on enthusiasts' specials. Preserved BR Standard class '5' 4-6-0 No. 73096 departs Yeovil Junction on 6th July, 2003 with the 'Cathedrals Express'. The engine will be serviced at Yeovil Steam Centre on the return journey later in the day. *Author*

Front cover: In its mixed traffic role, 'BB' class 4-6-2 No. 34069 *Hawkinge*, with a down West of England freight, takes water in the down platform road at Yeovil Junction on 22nd July 1958. The right of the photograph is framed by the massive lattice gantry supporting the down platform and down main starting signals, of which only the lower co-acting arms are visible. Mounted on the footbridge is the banner repeater for the up through road starting signal. *R.C. Riley*

Rear cover, top: '4575' class 2-6-2 tank No. 5522 proceeds from Yeovil Pen Mill Shed towards the station in June 1958. Such was the topography of the setting that the shed and its cramped site was instantly recognisable. Across the background at shed roof level can be seen the earthworks of the Yeovil Junction-Yeovil Town branch. *Colour Rail*

Rear cover, bottom: Since its introduction in 1915 the auto-train was very much a part of the Yeovil scene until its demise in December 1964. 'M7' class 0-4-4T No. 30129 waits departure from Yeovil Town for Yeovil Junction with a Maunsell auto-set on 6th October, 1962. *R.C. Riley*

Opposite: A brace of LSWR 'T9' class 4-4-0 locomotives approach Yeovil Junction with a down express in 1908. Known as 'Greyhounds', the superpower of two gave a fast ride over the undulating Salisbury-Exeter line. *N. Pomfret Collection*

Published by The Oakwood Press (Usk), P.O. Box 13, Usk, Mon., NP15 1YS.
E-mail:oakwood-press@dial.pipex.com
Website:www.oakwood-press.dial.pipex.com

Contents

The unusual arrangements of the island platform at Yeovil Town gave easy cross connections for passengers wishing to change trains. On 16th July 1958, '45XX' class 2-6-2 tank No. 4562 has arrived with a Taunton-bound train from Yeovil Pen Mill, whilst on the right 'M7' class 0-4-4T No. 30131 with an auto-train waits to depart for Yeovil Junction. Any passenger who, for example, was travelling from Weymouth to Exeter would have made three changes by the time he had left Yeovil Junction! *H.C. Casserley*

'14XX' class 0-4-2 tank No. 1467 propels a Weymouth-bound auto-train away from Yeovil Pen Mill on 1st September, 1956. In the centre is the engine shed with the tracks leading to Yeovil Town on the right. *G.M. Stubbs*

Introduction

The course of railway history frequently bestowed upon towns of modest size a network of lines and stations far in excess of requirements - often because the place concerned developed as a junction, but sometimes simply as a result of rivalry as a number of independent companies sought to establish themselves in the district or to defend it from infiltration by other railways. To some extent Yeovil fell into both of these categories. Originally three companies and two gauges were involved in the complicated story, and this - allied to the fact that the network was never 'planned' as such but took shape in a piecemeal fashion - finally resulted in a smallish town with no less than four stations, only one of which was really convenient for those with business in the commercial centre. It has proved to be the sort of layout which even 'rationalisation' in the post-Beeching era has failed to deal with effectively, for it has been the main sorrow in the tale of Yeovil's railways that the only useful stations - Yeovil Town for shoppers and office workers and Hendford Halt for factory employees - have been the ones to close, leaving only Yeovil Junction, more than two miles to the south of the town, and Pen Mill which stands on the Borough's eastern periphery.

The present arrangement of ill-placed stations means that there is practically no local rail business, despite Yeovil's importance as the industrial and commercial hub of a large area. Furthermore, the inconvenient crossroads arrangement of the two surviving lines discourages junction business, especially since the withdrawal of any form of connecting service between them, and for much of the time the two stations are quite deserted.

Yet all the stations were once very busy. The author recalls the time when Yeovil was an oasis of activity in the calm of a Winter Sunday, and the refreshment rooms at the Junction and Town stations were about the only place anywhere in the area where a warming cup of tea could be purchased - and very welcome it was when we enthusiasts had not yet progressed to cars and made our photographic expeditions by motor cycle! Even on those days, when Weymouth and even the larger railway centres such as Westbury were pervaded by Sabbath tranquillity, the signalman at Yeovil Town always seemed to be occupied with engine movements to and from the shed and shunting was generally in progress.

Indeed, the Yeovil area attracted photographers and enthusiasts from far and wide. We considered it worth our while to make the journey thither in order to see the long expresses of the Waterloo-Exeter line, or to find out what unusual specimens of motive power lurked in the shadows of the engine shed. There was always something going on, and we marvelled at the way in which the heavy traffic was handled within the cramped and inconvenient layouts of Pen Mill and Town stations. Hendford - once the terminus of the Salisbury & Yeovil and the first station in the town - had long since been nothing more than an unstaffed halt, but the goods yard was busy and the passenger trains that served it were well patronised, but 'Junction' - with its through lines for fast trains, two signal boxes, and spacious sidings - was the only Yeovil station to posses a truly 'Main Line' atmosphere. Despite being situated on a main line of the mighty GWR, Pen Mill seemed more typical of a secondary route.

It had to be admitted that, from the passengers' point of view, the arrangement was far from ideal. To change between a train on the Weymouth line and one of the Exeter services involved three changes - at Pen Mill, Town, and Junction - sometimes with lengthy waits at each, and parcels and goods transfers had perforce to follow the same devious route. It does indeed seem very strange that through the long years of rival railway companies, the Grouping, Nationalisation, and back again to private ownership, nothing has ever been done to make the lot of the transferring passenger any easier, despite much talk, many abortive suggestions, and the comparative ease with which better arrangements could be made. Perhaps the nearest to a satisfactory solution was achieved during the short time when the shuttle service ran directly between Junction and Pen Mill stations - although even this was of little use to anyone having business in the town centre. It is usual today to lay all the blame for this problem at the doors of the original 19th century promoters, but in the case of Yeovil they were victims of topography. It would have been impossible to build through lines between either Salisbury and Exeter or Frome and Weymouth that passed anywhere near the centre of Yeovil without much tunnelling and other heavy earthworks, the valleys dictating the routes adopted. The area is generally hilly, and only the old Bristol and Exeter line from Durston which, for much of its length traversed the Somerset Levels, approached the town without undue difficulty. The others had to be content with remote stations as they followed the rivers, and Yeovil found itself dumped on the end of a branch line as far as the LSWR was concerned instead of benefiting from direct access to the main West-of-England trains.

The story of Yeovil's railways is long and complex. Previous authors have written on the individual lines but the aim of this work is to bring all the various aspects together under one cover as a complete history. Yeovil not being at the end of a branch it has been necessary to include a certain amount of detail concerning the three railways and the lines that formed the routes into the town. Likewise matters of a National nature are explained to give readers the reasons for the changing circumstances affecting the railway.

Owning to the fact that four separate railway companies reached the town the story is broken up to cover those various early proposed schemes which failed, followed by the arrangements of the companies that were successful in constructing a line, in order of their construction and arrival. Finally, the narrative continues as one dealing with all events in chronological order - with the odd digression!

To add to the confusion both Town and Pen Mill stations were originally both called simply 'Yeovil', so in an attempt to improve clarity each station is referred to by its full name throughout the narrative. Wilts, Somerset & Weymouth is often used to describe the former GWR line to Weymouth.

During the existence of the broad gauge the standard (or 4 ft 8½ in. gauge) was often referred to as the 'narrow gauge', but in this account the term 'standard gauge' will be used.

To describe fully all the classes of engine that have appeared in the area over the years would seriously unbalance the text of this publication. Therefore general locomotive matters are described in the main narrative whilst the locomotive chapter deals with engines of a more local nature. Students of locomotive history and those wishing to study details of particular classes should consult the series of books published by the RCTS which are invaluable - particularly the detailed works of the late D.L. Bradley covering the Southern Group of companies.

The research into this work has brought a fresh awareness to many things that were taken for granted. Indeed, many things should have been better recorded before time and fading memories obscured them forever. Today, although railways do not play such an important part in the life of the community, Yeovil is a thriving town with Westland's as the principal employer. The year 2003 has already seen the local football club (The Glovers) become champions of the Nationwide Conference league and gain entry into division three of the Football League.

Unlike most branch line histories where the entire line can be referred to in the past tense, Yeovil is still alive, but in an uncertain world where policies change overnight there can be no definitive ending. It has survived Beeching and a host of other difficulties. We can but wish it well in its 150th year.

This book is dedicated to all the railwaymen who over the years served at Yeovil.

I am thinking of you at
YEOVIL JUNCTION.

A delightful period postcard sold at Yeovil Junction. How many of these were sent over the years, with news of pending arrivals, hope and joy, or sadly after 1914 perhaps the last message sent! This and other cards of its type, highlight the importance of the railway for travel and communication over the passing years. *Author's Collection*

Yeovil Town station and the north-east end of the town as seen from Summerhouse Hill in 1953. The development that had taken place northwards in the previous 50 years is evident when compared with the photograph on page 86. Likewise 50 years later the foreground of this picture is completely altered with the redevelopment of the former station area.

G.M. Stubbs

Chapter One

The Borough of Yeovil

There is evidence that early man resided in the Yeovil area, Bronze Age artefacts having been discovered on Wyndham Hill and Hendford Hill, and there are numerous examples of Roman discoveries in the area. Later a Saxon Hundred existed in the area and by 950 AD a Saxon church is known to have existed. Following the Norman Conquest the Domesday survey of 1086 referred to Yeovil by the names 'Ivel' or 'Givele' (pronounced Yivel), which later developed into a small self-governing borough that was separated from the Manor of Hendford by the time of the 12th century. The borough was placed under the Lordship of the Rector of St John's Church, with the daily civil administration in the hands of burgesses with a Portreeve as its head.

Prior to 1420 the borough came under the protection of the Maltravers family, the Lords of Hendford Manor. It was then granted by King Henry V to the Convent of Syon in Middlesex, but at the dissolution of the monasteries it reverted to the Crown and was eventually sold to Sir Edward Phelips of Montacute House in 1611, remaining in the ownership of that family until 1846.

The Black Death took its toll on Yeovil residents, and two devastating fires caused the loss of many dwellings in both 1623 and 1640. The outbreak of the Civil War in 1642 saw Yeovil on the side of the Earl of Bedford, who besieged the King's forces under the Marquis of Hertford in Sherborne Castle with a force of 7,000. Following several indecisive skirmishes, the Earl, whilst garrisoned in Yeovil, received news that the Marquis's troops had gathered on the hill to the east of the town and mustered his forces. The ensuing battle of Babylon Hill forced the Royalist Army to retreat back into Sherborne Castle.

Later the Plague caused more death and suffering. In 1647 it was reported that many hundreds had died and that no one would undertake to bury them. Under Oliver Cromwell Yeovil had not been a prosperous or happy place; but the restoration of the monarchy under Charles II in 1660 brought forth a new prosperity to the town as agriculture and the market flourished. From 1753 the Yeovil Turnpike Company serviced roads leading into the town.

The Beauties of England, published in 1776, described Yeovil thus: 'This is a good large town and a great thoroughfare on the post road to Cornwall. The streets are narrow and the houses for the most part mean. There is a manufacture of cloth here, but the principal one is for gloves'. Leather dressing and tanning had long been carried on in the town, and well before 1800 the sewing of gloves provided work for local women and children who often worked from their homes. The census of 1801 gave a population of 2,774 for the parish of Yeovil, which contained at least 20 farms and extended from Yeovil Marsh to Key Farm, on the Dorchester Road, and from Vagg to the River Yeo at Lyde. The weekly market at the 'Borough' sold the agricultural products of the surrounding villages and also traded in flax and hemp - the raw materials of the local textile industry. The decline in the use of sails by ships as they turned to steam power caused a dwindling demand for both sailcloth and rope and the industry gradually declined, but there was a brief upturn during World War I. At the end of hostilities there was a final recession during which Bunford Flax Mill eventually closed, thus bringing to an end a local industry.

As Yeovil expanded it was clear that some form of local government was required. Following meetings of prominent townspeople during 1828 a Parliamentary Bill entitled 'An Act for paving, lighting, watching, watering, cleansing, repairing and widening and otherwise improving the streets, lanes and other public passages and places within the town of Yeovil and for regulating the Police thereof' was drafted, this receiving the Royal Assent in June 1830. It paved the way for the formation of modern Yeovil, the population of the town having almost doubled in the previous 20 years.

The textile trade had drastically declined by the time the first railway arrived in 1853, an event which opened up the possibilities of new industries and allowed the town's products to be supplied to a wider world. Following much local political infighting, the 'Yeovil Improvements Bill' received the Royal Assent on 3rd July, 1854 and Yeovil became a Municipal Borough in its own right.

The arrival of the town's first railway the previous year brought fresh prosperity to the area as a wider market quickly developed. In 1856 it was reported that 421,000 pairs of gloves were manufactured, and in the same year Daniel Vickery wrote,

Yeovil's present bustling streets bear little resemblance to their former state, and Hendford once so quiet in its outward appearance, and hearing so rarely a stranger's footfall, is now become the most noisy and frequently trodden part of the town.

By 1861 the population had risen to 8,486 and two other railway routes had opened to allow easy rail access to all parts of the country. The tanning and glove-making industries that had been carried on in the area since the 14th century expanded and reached their peak by the turn of the century. In 1952, 50 per cent of gloves manufactured in England were produced in Yeovil, but following the importation of foreign goods the last glove factory closed in 1989, although the leather goods firm of Pittards continues to flourish.

During 1888 Messrs Aplin & Barrett established their Western Counties Creameries, and 10 years later their premises in Newton Road were well established. In 1901, adopting the 'St Ivel' brand name, they became for over half a century one of the leading producers of soft cheeses and other food products, until absorbed into the United Dairies group who eventually closed the Yeovil factory.

Fortunately another industry developed, at first slowly. J.B. Petter had commenced trade as an ironmonger with premises in the Borough, being involved in the manufacture of agricultural implements. Electrical work was also undertaken. In 1888 the PS *Monarch*, a Weymouth paddle steamer, was equipped with electric light by Messrs Petter. The firm then received nationwide recognition for the invention and production of the 'Nautilus' fire grate. In 1895 experiments were made when a one-horse-power petrol engine was installed in a horseless carriage, but although this project failed the production of a range of stationary oil engines commenced at the Nautilus works in Reckleford, which proved to be highly successful over the years. During 1926 Petter's and one of their former apprentices, Douglas Seaton,

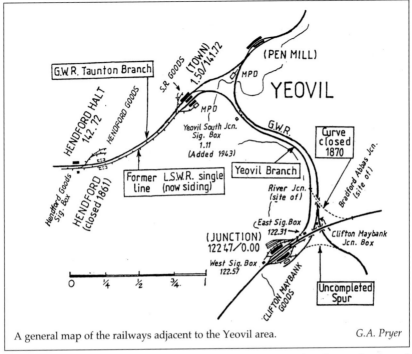

A general map of the railways adjacent to the Yeovil area.   G.A. Pryer

commenced the production of the Petter - Seaton car but after the production of 18 models the project was abandoned. If events had swung the other way Yeovil could well have become the Dagenham or Longbridge of the West!

However, other developments were to thrust Yeovil into the forefront of technology. In 1913 a new factory was constructed at Westland and after the outbreak of war aircraft production commenced in August 1915, the first completed machine - a Short 184 float-plane - leaving Yeovil by rail on 1st January, 1916. The war years saw production forge ahead, 1,000 aircraft being produced between 1915 and 1918. Fortunately through difficult times in the following years the company won many orders. In 1935 the aircraft works ceased to be a branch of Petter's Ltd, and as 'Westland Aircraft Ltd' the company moved forward again to construct over 2,400 aircraft during World War II.

On Thursday 24th April, 1947 aviation history was made when a Sikorsky helicopter took off from Westland's airfield. Having gained the manufacturing rights of the Sikorsky helicopter in October 1948 their first helicopter a - Westland Dragonfly - made its maiden flight. Westland's quickly secured a good section of the helicopter market and withdrew from constructing fixed wing aircraft. Today Westland's (as the company is now known) is the principal employer in the town.

The town has seen vast changes in the past 50 years. Many of the old narrow streets and associated houses have been demolished and dual carriageways constructed through part of the town, with car parks and new shops built bringing the former small town into the 20th century. The changes in local government in 1974 saw the end of the old Yeovil Borough Council, amalgamation with various local rural districts producing a new Yeovil District Council, since renamed South Somerset District Council.

General arrangement drawing of railways within the Yeovil area

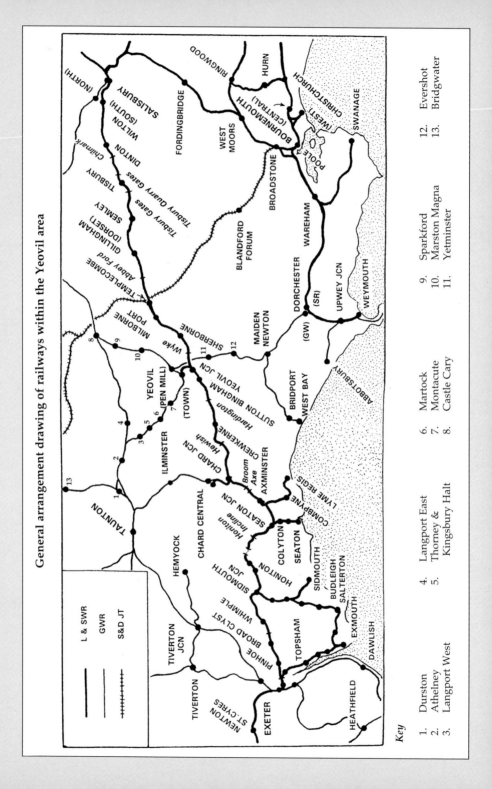

Key

L & SWR

GWR

S&D JT

1. Durston
2. Athelney
3. Langport West
4. Langport East
5. Thorney & Kingsbury Halt
6. Martock
7. Montacute
8. Castle Cary
9. Sparkford
10. Marston Magna
11. Yetminster
12. Evershot
13. Bridgwater

Chapter Two

The Race to the West
and the Battle of the Gauges

For a town of its size, the railway system of Yeovil has always been complicated. It was a crossroads of routes; the product of companies who - in their early days - were engaged in a battle of territorial rights and the Gauge War. The main contestants were the Bristol & Exeter Railway, the Wilts, Somerset & Weymouth Railway and the London & South Western Railway, the former two being of broad gauge (7 ft) the latter the standard gauge (4 ft 8½ in.).

Before describing the details of the three principal participating companies, a general description of the various proposed early schemes has to be considered.

South Somerset and Dorset were extremely rural, only Weymouth and Poole being large centres of population. Both towns were ancient seaports which had recently lost trade to the newly rail connected port of Southampton, whilst to the East of the County Bournemouth did not even exist at that time. The Great Western Railway (GWR) had completed its line from Paddington to Bristol in June 1841 and the Bristol & Exeter Company extended the route to Taunton and on to Exeter by May 1844, whilst to the East the London & Southampton Railway - later to become the London & South Western Railway (LSWR) - had completed its line from London to Southampton in 1839. Thus with the broad gauge lines skirting around the North of Somerset before cutting across to Taunton and the Devon border, and the standard gauge ending at Southampton, much of the counties of Wiltshire, Somerset, Dorset, and the western part of Hampshire were ripe for railway development. More importantly, virtually the whole of Devon and westwards into Cornwall (where Falmouth was still an important mail packet port) were without railways. It was also Government policy to encourage a line of railway to Plymouth along the channel coast as part of the defences against invasion.

It was against this backdrop that the various schemes were formulated, some planned as extensions of either the Great Western and London & Southampton railways even before they were completed. Those in which Yeovil would have been directly or indirectly involved are as follows. Firstly in 1836 a scheme was put before Parliament for The Bath & Great Western Union Railway, leaving the Great Western at Bath and proceeding to Weymouth via Wincanton, Cerne Abbas, and Dorchester. With its intended extension to Weymouth Harbour, it was clearly a scheme to open Weymouth up as a channel port. However, as it came at a time when work on the Great Western proper had only just commenced it was premature and was withdrawn from Parliament. Although passing to the east of Yeovil, if constructed it could well have changed the course of future events.

In the same year a company was formed under the title of 'The South Western Railway' (no connection with the later London & South Western Railway). The engineer was none other than George Stephenson, who projected a line joining the then under construction London & Southampton Railway west of Basingstoke at Worting. It would have passed through Overton but missed the important market town of Andover before continuing through Stockbridge and Horsebridge - from where a branch would have cut back onto the London & Southampton line at Hook Pit, near Kings Worthy thence westwards to Salisbury, Tisbury, Gillingham and Stalbridge, keeping some 3-4 miles south of Templecombe and Sherborne before reaching Yeovil. It would then have run via Martock before joining the proposed Bristol & Exeter Railway at Bathpool, east of Taunton. At that time no decision had been made as to the gauge of the Bristol & Exeter line. It was revealed at a meeting of the South Western Company that the new Parliamentary Standing Orders of 1837 would render it necessary to dissolve the company, a process that was carried out. Had the scheme proceeded it is interesting to speculate what effect the 99½ mile line would have had on the future railway development of Yeovil and indeed the entire West of England! Also during 1836 the London, Salisbury, Exeter and Falmouth Railway was proposed, with two branches from Queen Camel to serve Sherborne and Yeovil, but again the Bill was withdrawn.

Towards the end of 1844 four schemes were proposed, three of which affected Yeovil. The LSWR, which had obtained powers to construct a line from Bishopstoke (now known as Eastleigh) to Salisbury proposed an extension westwards as 'The South Western Extension Railway' to Yeovil via Gillingham, Templecombe, and Sherborne. The Bristol & Exeter Railway proposed a line from a junction at Durston (between Bridgwater and Taunton) to Yeovil and thence to Weymouth.

Thirdly the Wilts & Somerset Railway, a local concern supported by the Great Western, planned to build a broad gauge line from a junction at Thingley (near Corsham, on the Paddington - Bristol main line) to Salisbury, where it would meet the LSWR branch from Bishopstoke (Eastleigh) and thus provide connections to Southampton and the South Coast. There were also to be branches to Devizes, Bradford-on-Avon, and Frome with a mineral branch to Radstock.

The first meeting of the company was held at Warminster on 9th July, 1844, at which I.K. Brunel submitted plans with an estimate of £650,000 to cover all costs for the construction of the line. The committee decided that the capital of £650,000 be divided into 13,000 £150 shares and that a deposit of £2 10s. be paid on every share taken up. The Secretary of the GWR, Charles Saunders, explained to the meeting two schemes whereby the GWR would stand as guarantors of a fixed percentage, Wilts & Somerset subscribers being pledged from GWR funds 3½ per cent on capital and after paying that amount, any surplus being equally divided between Wilts & Somerset shareholders and the GWR; or the investors to receive on each £50 share, half the dividend payable on a GWR share of the same value, with a guarantee that it would never be less than 3½ per cent per annum on capital. Of course this generous offer was not without strings! In consideration of these payments to be made to the shareholders, the GWR would be lessees of the line, and they were prepared to subscribe up to half the capital required.

The Wilts & Somerset committee accepted the second scheme, in return for which the GWR would have a perpetual lease and rights to work the line. In an effort to raise local subscriptions, during August the GWR announced that they would raise the guarantee offer to 4 per cent.

The following month it was decided to extend the line from Frome to Yeovil and connect with the proposed Bristol & Exeter Company line from Durston to Weymouth, this being approved by the Board of Trade, Brunel estimating that a further £350,000 would cover the extra cost. However, events were moving ahead with other schemes, and at an October meeting it was announced that the Bristol & Exeter company now wished to terminate its branch from Durston at Yeovil and not proceed to Weymouth. The GWR and the Wilts & Somerset, with the sanction of the Board of Trade, then decided to extend their line to Weymouth with branches from Yeovil to Sherborne and from Maiden Newton to Bridport, and Brunel estimated the additional cost of this extension at £½m. Now, with the original objectives of the railway changed, it was decided that from the date of that meeting, 23rd October, 1844, the company would be known as the 'Wilts, Somerset & Weymouth Railway'.

Weymouth supported the scheme at a public meeting held on 30th October, 1844 and on 19th November GWR Directors subscribed on their company's behalf for 10,000 shares. By then Radstock colliery owners had pressed for the Radstock branch to be extended to Timsbury and join the GWR main line west of Bath at Twerton, but the provisional committee were not in favour of either this or a proposal to extend the Bradford-on-Avon branch to join the main line east of Bath. The Bristol & Gloucester Railway threatened that unless a direct connection was constructed it would oppose the Bill, resulting in the GWR reluctantly agreeing to an extension from Bradford-on-Avon to join the main line at Bathampton.

Thus at the end of 1844 the stage was set for the Wilts, Somerset & Weymouth Railway to apply to Parliament for its Act, the Board of Trade being in favour subject to an application in a future session for a direct line to either Bath or Bristol. The Wilts, Somerset & Weymouth Railway Act was passed on 30th June, 1845 for the line as planned, the gauge to be that of the GWR which was to lease the line. The authorised capital was £1½m with borrowing powers of £½m. Yeovil's second railway had been born, although it was to have a very difficult childhood!

The LSWR obtained an Act of Parliament on 4th July, 1844 to construct a 21 mile branch leaving its London-Southampton line at Bishopstoke (Eastleigh) to Salisbury. Terminating east of the city at Milford, this new line opened to goods traffic on 27th January, 1847 and passenger traffic on 1st March. Although not offering the most direct route from London, it was a major step forward in the South Western's expansion to the West and was later to form an important route to Southampton and Portsmouth from Wales and the North West.

The Southampton & Dorchester Railway proposed to construct a line from Southampton to Dorchester via Ringwood and Wimborne, Moorsom, the company Engineer, having his own agenda for future expansion. Although not directly connected with Yeovil, its construction was to have an influence on future schemes, especially the later 'Central Route' to Exeter.

Plans were deposited on 30th November, 1845 for the 'Great West of England or South Western Extension Railway', to run from a junction with the Bristol & Exeter at Bathpool (in the parish of West Monkton), then in a south-east direction through Ruishton, Hatch Beauchamp, Isle Abbots, South Petherton,

Martock, Stoke Under Ham (Stoke Sub Hamdon), Montacute and Yeovil, thence through the counties of Dorset and Wiltshire to Salisbury to form a junction with the London & Southampton Railway at Kings Worthy, near Winchester. Again these plans were not proceeded with, but had they been, this line would have been an all-embracing cross-country route of significant value to the Yeovil and South Somerset area.

The 1840s saw the promotion of railways on such a scale that the period became known as the 'Railway Mania'. Some of the proposed projects were excellent, others mediocre, whilst others were nothing but wild speculation with little prospect of commercial success. Indeed, so prolific were the plans that it was said at the time that, a few established companies apart, the only money being made out of railways was lining the pockets of solicitors and land agents!

Little else developed until 1844 by which time the country was well and truly in the grip of the 'Railway Mania' and the Government decided to step in. It had been suggested that the railways be nationalised, but it was to be over 100 years before this was to happen. A committee was appointed to examine all railway projects so that unnecessary duplication of routes could be avoided and valuable Parliamentary time would not be wasted on Bills for schemes that had no chance of succeeding. The Committee known as the 'Five Kings' was chaired by Earl Dalhousie, and for the next few years the decisions of these gentlemen were to have a great impact on railway development throughout Great Britain.

Amongst the decisions made which favoured the broad gauge were those concerning the four 1844 proposals, the companies coming to an agreement that was signed on 16th January, 1845. The South Western abandoned its extensions west of Salisbury and undertook not to promote any lines west of either Salisbury or Dorchester. The Great Western gave up its option on the Southampton & Dorchester, which was to be constructed to standard gauge. The Bills had an easy passage through Parliament, the Wilts, Somerset & Weymouth Bill was passed on 30th June, 1845, the Southampton & Dorchester on 21st July, and the Bristol & Exeter on 31st July. The Salisbury-Yeovil line was dropped as a result of the agreement. The decision of the Five Kings was only classed as a 'recommendation', which was to have later ramifications as within months the agreement was ignored.

The tip of the iceberg was the Southampton & Dorchester Company's Weymouth branch proposed in 1845, which would have approached the town from the east after leaving the main line at Moreton. Although Weymouth is not exactly 'west' of Dorchester, the company clearly wished to deprive the Wilts, Somerset & Weymouth from having a monopoly of the port.

Meanwhile on the borders of Dorset and Somerset everybody threw their hats into the ring, the London, Salisbury & Yeovil Junction Railway was promoted to build a line from Basingstoke to Sutton Bingham with a short branch to serve Yeovil. Promoted at the same time was the Exeter, Yeovil & Dorchester Railway, with a branch from near Crewkerne to Bridport where it would join the proposed Bridport Railway giving access to Dorchester via Maiden Newton. As these lines from Bridport to Maiden Newton and on to

In the meantime work had commenced on the Yeovil branch, the contracts having been agreed early in 1847 when Messrs Rigby commenced on the earthworks between Yeovil and Martock, Added to the many problems that beset railway construction at that period it was discovered that wells at Brympton and Houndstone ran dry as a result of the construction of the nearby railway cutting, whilst at Yeovil the town watchmen requested and were granted an extra 1s. on account of the number of navvies frequenting the town. Work on this six miles, which contained the only heavy earthworks on the branch, was completed within two years. However, the financial situation - created mainly by the company having to purchase locomotives and rolling stock - caused work to be suspended.

The uncompleted works remained until April 1852 when the Board authorized assistance for the Engineer to prepare working plans for the Yeovil branch. Both Mr Fox, the Engineer, and the Secretary with Mr Brunel were requested on 5th May to attended a Board meeting where the Engineer presented plans which were approved, showing the position of stations on the branch and the junction with the proposed Wilts, Somerset & Weymouth Railway at Pen Mill, Yeovil.

On 1st May the tenders for the Yeovil branch were opened. The Engineer had estimated the total cost to be £130,646 1s. 1d. and the tenders were as follows:

William Peniston	£106,000
Waring Bros	£103,650
Hutchinson & Ritson	£99,200
(£70,000 if Barlow rails were used)	
J. & C. Rigby	£96,566
Robert Sharpe	£94,530 6s. 10d.
Richard Stone	£94,000
J.W. Harvey	£87,987
Thomas Davies	£82,288
William Baker	£81,000

The Board accepted the tender of William Baker for £81,000, but at a meeting on 21st May a letter was read from Baker declining to enter into the contract for that sum and asking for an additional £5,000, whereupon the Board decided to offer the contract to those who had previously tendered. The Engineer attended the Board meeting on 26th May when he presented a new estimate for the construction of the branch of £92,290, and the new tenders were then opened as follows:

J. & C. Rigby	£89,000
Lansdell & Stone	£87,500
William Baker	£86,950
J. & W. Harvey	£86,841 10s.
Hutchinson & Ritson	£86,000
(£92,000 if Barlow rails used supplied by the contractors)	
Thomas Davies	£85,994

The Board accepted the tender of Messrs Hutchinson & Ritson for £86,000 for the construction of the branch.

Work commenced in June 1852 on the remaining 13 miles to Durston. The *Western Flying Post* for 8th June, 1852 reported:

> Yeovil & Durston Railway. The works on this line are now progressing with vigour, 150 men are engaged on the works, in the neighbourhood of Durston, the work is also progressing on other portions of the line. We may now look forward to the completion at a very not too distant period.

For work completed by 4th September the contractors received a payment of £3,691, and that November they offered to construct the stations on the branch. However, they were delayed by heavy winter flooding (at the time a regular occurrence in the area), and work was not completed until the following year with stations at Durston, Athelney, Langport, Martock and Yeovil.

In December 1852 it was recorded that the Traffic Department required additional stock for the Yeovil branch: two first class, two composites, six second class, and four third class carriages. Orders for their construction were given, but they were not ready for the opening of the branch. Indeed, these actual vehicles may never have worked on the branch at all!

It is worth mentioning at this point that the coaches of the 1850-1860 period were far removed even from those of the turn of the century, usually being mounted on six-wheeled underframes, short in length and with small compartments. Third class had only unupholstered wooden seats, and lighting was by means of an oil lamp suspended in the roof. On the Bristol & Exeter the livery was gloomy. Originally the passenger stock was dark crimson lake, after 1867 changing to dark brown, only to be changed to light brown upper panels and dark brown lower panels in 1870 and then again to a single brown shade.

On Saturday 12th February, 1853 fire completely destroyed the workshops and a majority of the timber supplies at the contractor's yard at Somerset Bridge near Bridgwater, but despite this setback in March Mr Ritson attended a Board meeting and proposed a premium for opening the Yeovil branch by 16th August instead of the 1st November. But at a meeting later in the month he was informed that the Board could not accept his terms.

However, all was completed by late September, and on Friday 23rd the line was inspected by Lieut Tyler RE of the Board of Trade accompanied by the Bristol & Exeter company Secretary, the Engineer, the superintendent of locomotives and the superintendent of traffic.

The wording of the report gives a good description of the works as follows:

> The branch is 18 miles 49 chains in length from the junction with the Bristol & Exeter Railway at Durston to the station at Yeovil, but the portion of railway which the company wish now to open for public traffic extends 12 chains further to a crossing place under a bridge called Hendford Bridge, in order to enable the engine to be disengaged from the carriages on arrival at Yeovil, and I have therefore included that portion in my inspection.
>
> This line has been laid single with sidings at two of the intermediate stations only, but land has been purchased for the purpose of constructing a double line at a future period. The gauge is the same as that of the Bristol & Exeter Railway, 7 ft 2½ in. from centre to centre of the rails, the weight of the rails is 60lb. per yard, and they are on longitudinal sleepers averaging 14 in. x 7 in. and 21 ft in length, connected by transoms 15 ft apart and 7 in. x 5 in. The transoms are secured to the sleepers by iron strap bolts.

Advert for tenders for the construction of stations along the Durston-Yeovil branch, *Western Flying Post*, 1st March 1853.

Western Gazette

A considerable goods as well as passenger traffic is anticipated to Yeovil, but the principal part of the former is intended to be brought to Langport (a station 7 miles from Durston) by water, and to be taken thence by rail to Yeovil. A great part of the line traverses the moors, which are in many places of a boggy nature and subject to floods, but as 58 aqueducts or large culverts have been constructed on piles driven generally from 40 to 50 ft deep, I do not anticipate any danger from the latter source.

I observed however that portions of the embankments were not sufficiently firm to warrant traffic at a high speed over them. As far as I can see there has not been much difficulty in obtaining a foundation for the embankments excepting at one spot, where the peat was considerably elevated at each side of the railway and where fasciones & faggots had been inserted as a remedial measure. Under all the circumstances I would beg to recommend to the company that they should not on any account allow a speed of 20 miles an hour to be exceeded over this portion, and over the embankments which occur between 1 mile 49 chains, and 3 miles 34 chains, and between 4 miles 2 chains and 6 miles 33 chains from Durston.

The under bridges over roads are 5 in number they are all of masonry and of spans varying from 10 to 20 ft. The over bridges are 18 in number 10 being constructed with timber girders and the remainder entirely of masonry, the spans of the former vary from 30 ft on the square to 30 ft on the rgicase (?) and 36 ft on the skew and the latter from 30 ft to 79 ft.

These bridges appear to be substantially constructed with one exception, viz the flying arch over the railway to carry the Ilminster Road at 16 miles 32 chains from the fixed point near Durston, it is of a span of 65 ft on the square and 79 ft on the skew and has cracked on both spandrels apparently in consequence of the south abutment not receiving sufficient support from the made earth in the rear. I am told that it has stood for 3 years in its present state, but I am of opinion that it should still be carefully watched and this, the engineer of the line promises shall be carried out.

Over the rivers Tone and Parrett are two viaducts, the centre span of the former is 35 ft on the square and 40 ft on the skew, and of the latter 47 ft on the square and 50 ft on the skew. Their construction is peculiar in as much as the permanent way is carried on three beams, eight foot apart, the two exterior beams being trussed and connected with wrought iron rods and cast iron shoes, and the centre beam being supported by wrought iron tension rods attached to the ends of the 8 in planking which forms the floor of the bridge, and being thus partially carried by the exterior beams. The greatest deflections which I obtained from these viaducts with an engine and tender weighing together about 46 tons and attached to a smaller engine and tender, were from the Tone bridge $\frac{3}{8}$ in. and from the Parrett bridge $\frac{7}{16}$. The safety of these viaducts will principally depend upon the screwing up of the nuts of the various tension rods from time to time.

In regard to the working of the line, I am informed that the goods traffic is to be carried on by night and the passenger traffic by day, and that no two engines on trains to be permitted under any circumstances to work on the line at the same time which is a very satisfactory arrangement and I beg to enclose a copy of the instructions to guards and others which has been issued.

As the monthly notice sent in by the company for the opening of the line does not expire until the 30th instant, I have deferred sending in the present report until the

Right: One of the numbered tickets issued for the public dinner held in Yeovil to celebrate the opening of the railway from Durston to Hendford on 1st October, 1853.

Leslie Brooke Collection

OPENING OF THE RAILWAY TO YEOVIL.

TICKET

FOR THE

Public Dinner, to be held at the Town Hall,

YEOVIL,

On Saturday, the 1st of October, 1853,

No. *140*

BRISTOL AND EXETER RAILWAY
YEOVIL BRANCH.
MARKET TRAINS.

THE Public are informed that on THURSDAYS, single 1st or 2nd class tickets taken to BRIDGWATER by the Train leaving

Yeovil	11.10 a.m.
Martock	11.30 a.m.
Langport	11.50 a.m.

will be available for the RETURN JOURNEY by any Train during the day.

On FRIDAYS, single 1st or 2nd class tickets taken to YEOVIL by the Train leaving

Bridgwater	9.10 a.m.
Taunton	8.51 a.m.
Durston	9.30 a.m.
Athelney	9.42 a.m.
Langport	10. 0 a.m.
Martock	10.20 a.m.

will be available for the Return Journey by any Train during the day.

On SATURDAYS, single 1st or 2nd class tickets taken to TAUNTON by the Train leaving

Yeovil	11.10 a.m.
Martock	11.30 a.m.
Langport	11.50 a.m.

will be available for the Return Journey by any Train during the day.

No luggage allowed.   Tickets not transferable.

By order of the Directors,

J. B. BADHAM, Secretary.

Bristol Terminus, 21st October, 1853.

Left: Advert for market day trains along the Durston-Yeovil branch, *Western Flying Post*, 25th October, 1853.   *Western Gazette*

Chapter Four

The Wilts, Somerset & Weymouth Railway

Work on construction of the Wilts, Somerset & Weymouth line had proceeded during the summer of 1846 with contracts let for various sections of the line throughout Wiltshire, Somerset and Dorset, and at a General Meeting held on 15th August, 1846 the Engineer reported that work had commenced on construction of the line between Westbury and Dorchester. The Directors, concerned about the spiritual needs of the navvies in the towns of Bruton and Yeovil and the surrounding villages, donated £75 to the Rector of West Camel to provide a railway chaplain, but his services were dispensed with in February 1848 in view of the few navvies working in the area. The aftermath of the railway mania found many schemes in difficulty, including the Wilts, Somerset & Weymouth where not only did it become difficult to raise fresh capital but there were many unpaid share calls. The double track section from Thingley Junction near Chippenham to Westbury opened on 5th September, 1848, at which point the financial situation caused the work to be stopped and the contractors dismissed leaving unfinished works across three counties! Work was restarted on the Westbury-Frome section and in January 1850 it was decided that it would not proceed beyond Frome on the Weymouth line and Warminster on the Salisbury branch. Work forged ahead on the Westbury-Frome section which was opened to traffic on 7th October, 1850, the section to Warminster opening the following September. The Wilts, Somerset & Weymouth company Directors held their last meeting on 25th March, 1850, the GWR then taking over the work. From the beginning the GWR had invested £545,000 in the scheme and guaranteed 4 per cent on the capital, the official transfer of the company being confirmed by Parliament on 3rd July, 1851, when the Wilts, Somerset & Weymouth company was dissolved, and the work became the responsibility of the Great Western Railway.

However, little progress was being made apart from on the Warminster section and the Radstock branch, and by October 1851 the earthworks in the Castle Cary area were reported as being overgrown with vegetation and embankments and cuttings standing in an uncompleted state. Very little work was proceeding on the southern section of the line. At Weymouth, men were paid off and only a token workforce was employed in the Evershot area at Holywell. There was to be action in the courts over the non-completion of the line as provided for in the Parliamentary Acts.

In May 1851 two contractors, Messrs Wythes and Tredwell, proposed that they complete a simple single line at their own expense with the assistance of a loan in stock or debentures from the GWR, who would then work the completed line. This course of action which was later to become common practice with small impecunious companies created railways known as 'Contractors Lines'.

Although interested in the proposal the GWR could not agree to the loan. They had heavy financial commitments with the construction of the

Birmingham and Wolverhampton Railway where they faced stiff opposition from the LNWR. Instead they enquired whether the contractors would carry out the work without the loan if the GWR released Wythes from his present contract, but the contractors would not agree to this resulting in Wythes receiving compensation and being released from his contract in the July.

In the meantime the *Sherborne Mercury* was putting forth the view that meetings should be called in towns along the route with the object of awakening the GWR to the need to complete the works, the paper having suggested at one point that the GWR had little intention of completing the Wilts, Somerset and Weymouth. It also took the view that if the company could not be persuaded to continue with the works the power of the courts should be applied.

Whilst these matters were being aired in the press interested parties in Weymouth were also looking into schemes to have the line completed, a meeting being held at the Guildhall, Weymouth, in July 1851 where a resolution was passed that a committee be appointed to communicate with the Directors of the GWR in an effort to complete the railway. A local solicitor, William Eliot, had discussions with a GWR Director on this matter, but few details of the manner in which it was to be achieved or the financing were ever made public.

A further public meeting was held at Weymouth that autumn at which it was decided that a deputation travel to Yeovil in support of a meeting to be held there.

In Yeovil, where work had also ceased on the Bristol & Exeter line from Durston, there was a general dissatisfaction at the progress of the lines then under construction or proposed. Notices appeared in the press with over 150 names of businessmen and gentlemen of Yeovil and the surrounding towns calling for support at a meeting to be held at Yeovil Town Hall on Friday 17th October. This meeting would nominate a committee to communicate with the Directors of the GWR respecting the completion of the Wilts, Somerset and Weymouth Railway line.

The meeting was very influential, about 500 persons being present including several Members of Parliament, many of the principal landowners along the line, and a great number of manufacturers, agriculturalists, traders, and other interested parties. There were also representives from Bruton, Marston Magna, and Weymouth, and from Martock and Montacute on the route of the still uncompleted Bristol & Exeter Railway.

Many of those present represented the glove and other industries of Yeovil who were having difficulty in reaching a wider market owing to the want of a railway, whilst the Weymouth deputation were interested in the completion of the line to bolster the shipping trade to the Channel Islands. Several eloquent speeches were made during the course of the evening, and there is little doubt that both the Yeovil and Weymouth meetings were the catalyst for the formation of a local company to raise the capital locally and complete the line to Weymouth.

Eliot had already obtained support and had prepared proposals to put forward to the GWR. He had also engaged the London legal firm of Currie, Woodgate and Williams to deal with the legal matters. The formation of the new company, to be known as the Frome, Yeovil & Weymouth Railway, was

On 31st July, 1854 an Act was granted allowing an extension of time to complete the works. Despite problems concerning the branch from Bradford Junction to Bathampton, the goods branch between Frome and Radstock opened on 14th November, 1854, thus allowing some revenue to be obtained principally moving coal from the Somerset coalfield. By January 1856 £1,433,000 had been spent on the various lines, but the GWR was obliged to forge ahead. The section from Warminster to Salisbury opened on 30th June, 1856, but as this was broad gauge it gave only limited prospects for through traffic on to the LSWR towards Southampton and Portsmouth where the introduction of steamships could provide valuable coal traffic.

Work was progressing on the 26 mile section between Frome and Yeovil, with stations at Witham, Bruton, Castle Cary, Sparkford and Marston Magna (Marston until 1895). The completed works to Yeovil were inspected on Saturday 9th August, 1856 by Col Yolland for the Board of Trade. He reported that the rails were of the 'Bridge' type laid on longitudinal sleepers secured by fang bolts, the transverse ties were 6 in. by 4½ inches fastened with wrought-iron strap bolts, and the ballast was stone and gravel laid between 1 ft 6 in. and 2 ft thick. Although the line was stated as being 'complete' the inspector found that none of the distant signals at the stations had been connected, clocks to face the line were required at all stations, small portions of fencing still needed completion, and in places the longitudinal sleepers required packing. At Yeovil the turntable was not yet in place and the station buildings were incomplete and, although a temporary junction had been formed with the Bristol & Exeter line from Hendford, no proper arrangements for a junction had been made. In the circumstances the inspector reported, 'That by reason of the incompleteness of the works, the opening of the Wilts, Somerset & Weymouth Railway for traffic will be attended with danger to the public using the same'. However, by the end of the month it would appear that the objections had been overcome, the GWR putting forth the argument that the junction with the Bristol & Exeter spur did not require inspection as it was beyond the temporary terminus!

The line opened to traffic on 1st September, 1856. No doubt owing to the long-delayed opening there was no civic demonstration for the opening of Yeovil's second railway, the first train departing from Yeovil to Frome at 6.45 am, hauled by 'Firefly' class 2-2-2 *Mercury*, and the first train from Frome arriving at 11.45 am. The local press reported, '. . . the arrival and departure of these trains being witnessed by a great number of people who had gathered at the station '. Horse buses from the Mermaid and Three Choughs Hotels in Yeovil and the Kings Arms, Sherborne awaited the arrival of the down train, and a Weymouth coach was also waiting for passengers.

Mr G. Roberts was appointed station master at the new station, which the press described as a commodious building, although not quite finished. The opening train service was of five trains each way daily and two on Sundays. A goods train service of one train each way daily commenced on 1st October.

Work was also progressing well on the Yeovil-Weymouth section. An advert appearing in the *Western Flying Post* during July 1856 drew attention to an auction at the railway yard Yetminster where contractor's equipment used by Messrs Hill, Richardson & Cooper was sold upon their completion of the Holywell contract.

Advert announcing the opening of the
GWR Wilts, Somerset & Weymouth line
through to Weymouth in January 1857,
Western Flying Post, 20th January, 1857.

Western Gazette

THIS DAY.

G R E A T   W E S T E R N   R A I L W A Y.
OPENING TO WEYMOUTH.

NOTICE is hereby given that, on and after
Tuesday, the 20th of January, the Line from
YEOVIL to WEYMOUTH will be OPENED for the con-
veyance of Passengers and Parcels.
Time Bills of the Trains and all other particulars may be
procured at any of the Stations.
By Order of the Directors,
C. A. SAUNDERS, Secretary.
Paddington Station, January 16th, 1857.

The remaining section to Weymouth was nearing completion, and by mid-October it was reported that works on the last section were progressing satisfactorily. The permanent way was laid up to Dorchester, and the stations were in a forward state.

The completed works of the Yeovil-Weymouth section were inspected by Col Yolland on Thursday 15th January, 1857. The Colonel - accompanied by the contractor, Mr Ritson - departed from Yeovil Pen Mill at 9.30 am on board the inspection engine, arriving at Weymouth at 3.30 pm. As on the Frome-Yeovil section, the line consisted of 'Bridge' rails of 60 lb. per yard secured by fang bolts onto longitudinal timbers of 12 inches by 8¼ inches square. The inspector noted that 'in consequence of the length and steepness of the inclines the line will require to be worked with very great care, due attention being paid to the sufficiency of brake power'.

The line beyond Yeovil opened for public service on Tuesday 20th January, 1857, the *Western Flying Post* commenting on the event remarked, 'The event although long delayed and long expected - took people somewhat by surprise, and there was not time to get any of the contemplated demonstrations arranged at the station', adding that 'of course the Dorchester and Weymouth coaches would cease to run, the horses are to be sold at Yeovil market'. The first train departed at 6.15 am from Weymouth hauled by *Otho* and arrived at Yeovil containing a few passengers from Weymouth and Dorchester, whilst the second train to arrive was the down train from Chippenham which arrived 15 minutes late at 9.15 am. Whereas before this train had terminated at Yeovil, for the first time it continued to Weymouth, GWR officials including Mr Saunders the Secretary, Mr Graham, traffic manager, Mr Ward, Engineer, and Mr Ritson the contractor were amongst others who availed themselves of a journey to Weymouth. The fares were single first class 4s. 6d., second class 3s. 6d. and third class 2s. 3d.

The stagecoach was no match for the newly opened railway, which took an average of 1 hour 15 minutes to cover the distance, whereas the road coach took something like four hours. Two days after the railway's opening an advert appeared in the *Dorset County Chronicle* when the 'Duke of Wellington' coach, which had latterly worked between Yeovil and Weymouth, was put up for sale. Within a few years the new railways were virtually to remove the stagecoach from the roads. The 11th November, 1857 saw the opening of the branch line between Maiden Newton and Bridport. Although not directly connected with the railways of Yeovil, it filled a further gap on the rapidly expanding map and provided additional traffic over the Wilts, Somerset & Weymouth line.

The next important step was to double the line over the steeply graded section between Yeovil and Evershot in which it had climbed 386 ft in 8½ miles, the last 4½ miles between Yetminster and the summit at Evershot having a gradient of 1 in 57. Operation of this section was already creating difficulties, trains often having to be split at Yeovil to proceed as two portions. The climb to Evershot had already been the scene of an accident on 27th March, 1858. A down goods had reached a point about two miles beyond Yetminster when the locomotive became incapable of hauling its 31 wagon load, so the train was divided and 16 wagons taken forward. After a further mile the train was again divided and five wagons detached, but unfortunately when they were uncoupled they ran back down the incline into the 15 wagons previously left standing. Two wagons were severely damaged, one being thrown off the rails, and a large number of transoms were damaged. Although brakes had been applied the force of the collision caused the wagons to be driven back nearly half a mile.

During the latter part of 1858 work commenced on laying the second line of rails which were to form the up line, the earthworks and bridges having been completed to accommodate this during the original construction. Although at least 500 tons of new rails were ordered from manufacturers, in the difficult financial situation timber that was being laid in the Frome area was transferred to the work. During August 1858 1,000 tons of rails and five miles of timber were purchased from the Oxford, Wolverhampton & Worcester Railway to complete the work which Captain George Ross R.E. of the Board of Trade inspected on 7th March, 1859.

The following month saw a fire destroy a portion of Pen Mill station on Monday 18th April - although accounts of the conflagration are a little vague, the matter not receiving full coverage in the local press, *Pullmans Weekly News* just stated 'About half past ten yesterday (Monday) morning a fire broke out at the GWR station. The whole of the offices on the up side of the station are destroyed, but hopes are entertained that the platform may be saved'. At a GWR Board meeting the following day the report was brief, 'Mr Graham reported that the Yeovil station had yesterday been destroyed by fire, which broke out in the roof, and it is supposed that it had been occasioned by the flue having become overheated, but no certain information could yet be procured as to the direct cause of the fire'. It is generally considered that the main damage was to buildings on the down side and the damage was reported as being made good for £390 - a considerable sum at the time! However, it was decided that after making the down platform safe only the up platform would be used, this being extended to accommodate the two trains. The station was then worked as a 'one sided station' - a not unusual practice at that period although it was fraught with shunting moves and other difficulties as the line was single north of Yeovil but double towards Evershot without a trailing crossover at the south end. This involved all down trains having to run off the single line into the up platform and having then to reverse back onto the single line to proceed

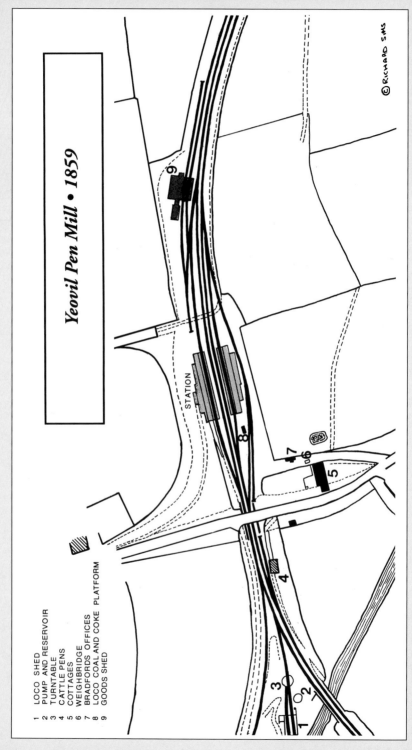

Yeovil Pen Mill • 1859

1 LOCO SHED
2 PUMP AND RESERVOIR
3 TURNTABLE
4 CATTLE PENS
5 COTTAGES
6 WEIGHBRIDGE
7 BRADFORDS OFFICES
8 LOCO COAL AND COKE PLATFORM
9 GOODS SHED

STATION

© RICHARD SIMS

Drawn and supplied by Richard Sims

Yeovil Pen Mill station 1859.

lines. The original scheme had included a branch to join the Wilts, Somerset & Weymouth Railway near its junction with the Bristol & Exeter line at Pen Mill.

The *Western Gazette* during March 1858 noted the marking out of the new line thus: 'It crosses the branch connecting the Bristol & Exeter, and Wilts, Somerset, & Weymouth Railways, and terminates near the back part of the Royal Osborne Brewery, where the station will be erected'. Shades of a previous scheme, if proceeded with it would have provided a terminal station at the foot of an incline and would have been completely impractical, only adding to the complex arrangements that developed in the area. This plan was quickly shelved in favour of a joint station, discussions taking place in August 1858 between the Salisbury & Yeovil company and the Bristol & Exeter Railway for the construction of a station to be situated on the Bristol & Exeter spur between Hendford and the Wilts, Somerset, & Weymouth station at Pen Mill. The fact that these negotiations had commenced without the LSWR being informed created a certain amount of ill feeling, but agreement was reached in June 1859 for a joint station at the foot of Newton Hill, on the east end of the town served by Middle Street. The new station was to be reached from a branch leaving the main line west of Bradford Abbas at a point later to be known as Bradford Abbas Junction, curving northwards to cross the Wilts, Somerset & Weymouth line before descending to run alongside the Weymouth line and finally turning west to meet the Bristol & Exeter company's Hendford-Pen Mill line.

At a company meeting held on 27th January, 1860 the question of providing a station for Yeovil was raised and, in order to expedite the building of this facility and complete the whole railway and works by the 1st May, it was resolved that a proposal be made to the LSWR that they should arrange the plans for the station with the Bristol & Exeter company and give immediate orders for its construction, and that the Salisbury & Yeovil company should pay over to the South Western Company such sum as (under agreement with them), that company would have had to expend on the construction of the station.

Delays in coming to an agreement and the short time available before the opening of the Salisbury & Yeovil were resolved by the simple expedient of laying a line of standard gauge rails alongside the Bristol & Exeter to Hendford, where a temporary LSWR platform was erected on the south side of the line. Likewise from the Exeter direction a curve was laid from the new Yeovil Junction station, curving northwards it joined the Bradford Abbas curve on the west side of the bridge over the Weymouth line at a point to be known as Upper Junction (also referred to as River Junction).

On 4th April Mr Fox, the Bristol & Exeter company Engineer, was instructed to lay an independent standard gauge line from the point of the proposed joint station to Hendford on the south side of the existing broad gauge track. Work was soon put in hand and 12 days later he reported back to the Board that he was fast proceeding with the standard gauge railway between the two points.

Money had already raised its ugly head when in January the Bristol & Exeter Board argued that 'inasmuch as this company had borne the whole expense of erecting the station at Hendford, the Board considers that a rent equal to 5 per cent on moiety of the outlay on that portion which may be used jointly should be paid to this company'.

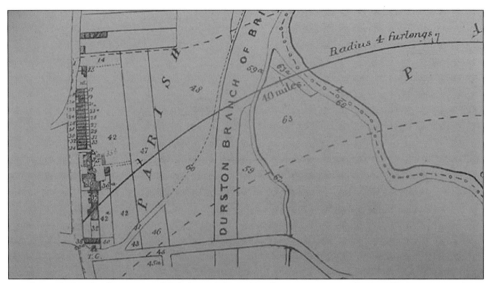

General plan for the proposed Salisbury & Yeovil Railway terminus in the Middle Street area of
the town, the present Newton Road going from left to right across the bottom of the map.

Had the original Salisbury & Yeovil Railway plans of 1854 proceeded their station could have
been situated on the left side of Middle Street at this point. A pre-1914 view shows the area, with
the Elephant & Castle Hotel on the left, the impressive *Western Gazette* office and printing works
built in 1906 is on the right, on the corner of Newton Road.   *Author's Collection*

The Bristol & Exeter company had also objected to the joint use of its engine shed and turntable at Hendford station. Although no reasons are recorded, the complications of having to convert both to mixed gauge plus the limited space in which both were situated would have been grounds enough! Mr Strapp, the LSWR Engineer, reported that the turntable at Sherborne could be moved temporarily to Yeovil at a cost of about £25, the LSWR Board later agreeing that this be carried out at their expense.

On Saturday 26th May Col Yolland of the Board of Trade inspected the section between Sherborne and Yeovil Junction and the section between Bradford Abbas Junction and Hendford. The best description of the new line is in the words of Col Yolland, which he reported on as follows:

A portion of the Salisbury & Yeovil railway which extends from the town of Sherborne to the junction with a new piece of line laid down on the narrow gauge by the Bristol & Exeter Railway Company in the Parish of Yeovil a length of 5 miles 37 chains.

The permanent way is precisely similar to that laid down on the other portions of the Salisbury & Yeovil Railway which I have already inspected and described in previous reports.

The line is single throughout, and without any sidings but the land has been purchased and the Bridges and Viaducts have been constructed for a double line if hereafter required. There are 3 over and 7 under bridges and four Viaducts, of the bridges six are entirely constructed of brick and stone with Bridgwater Lime and the remaining four have brick and stone abutments and iron girders, three of cast iron and one with wrought iron girders - the largest span being 30 ft on the square and 49 ft 10 in. on the skew for the wrought iron girders.

One of the viaducts over the River Yeo is composed of 5 arches, with cast iron arched girders the span being 49 ft on the square and 51 ft on the skew and four of 25 ft span built on brick and stone with Bridgwater Lime. The other viaducts are small with stone abutments and cast iron girders. The masonry of these works is good and substantial and the iron girders are sufficiently strong.

Until a joint station is erected at Yeovil for the use of the Bristol & Exeter and the Salisbury and Yeovil Railway Companies under the provisions of a Bill now before the legislature, the Salisbury & Yeovil Railway Company are to have the use of the Hendford station, but no arrangement has yet been made for the use of the engine table belonging to the Bristol & Exeter Railway Company at Hendford station.

The Salisbury & Yeovil company propose to make use of the triangle formed by the eastern and western fork and the main line (between them) from Exeter to Salisbury as a means of turning their engines for Yeovil station. This may be admitted as a temporary arrangement if the Bristol & Exeter turntable cannot be used but as local trains are to be run in each direction from Yeovil station, it will be necessary that an engine turntable should be erected in or close to the joint station in the course of the next three months.

Again as no station accommodation for passengers is provided at the present time at Yeovil for this company permission to open for public traffic must be made to depend on the erection of the signals required on the Bristol & Exeter New Line etc. up to Hendford station. When these are complete, and when undertakings have been given as regards running tender foremost and with reference to the mode of working proposed to be adopted their Lordships' sanction for the opening of the line may be given.

I have now however to report that by reason of the incompleteness of the works the opening of the Salisbury & Yeovil Railway between Sherborne and Yeovil cannot be sanctioned without danger to the public using the same.

It would appear that the main problem was the section of line from where the new joint station was later to be built and the Bristol & Exeter station at

Hendford. The standard gauge track was laid for much of its length alongside the existing broad gauge line between Pen Mill and Hendford and had been constructed by the Bristol & Exeter Company. Col Yolland was displeased with the fact that no details of the line's construction had been forwarded to the Board of Trade prior to him carrying out his inspection of which he reported:

> The line is not very long and there are no works of any importance on it - and it is in good order - but there are distant signals still required to be erected to cover Hendford station - one on this new line, one on the side towards Durston - and, in the event of a pair of points of a crossover road, situated near the station signal east of Hendford station not being kept locked, then a third distant signal will be wanted on the branch to the Wilts, Somerset and Weymouth station.
>
> The projecting knobs of the stone sidewall on the south side of an over bridge near the station signal must be removed, as the rails are little above 3 feet from the side of the wall.
>
> I have thereby to report that the opening of this portion of new line for traffic cannot by reason of the incompleteness of the works, be sanctioned without danger to the public using the same.

The railway companies were informed that the opening would be postponed for a month. Without delay the Bristol & Exeter wrote to the Board of Trade apologising for its tardiness in supplying details of the new works. Concerning the other defects the letter stated, 'In reference to the requirements of the additional signals, they either are or will be erected before 1st June, as they were ordered to be erected immediately upon hearing Col Yolland's opinion that they were necessary'.

Meanwhile the Salisbury & Yeovil was taking measures to ensure that there was no delay in opening, a letter to the Board of Trade promising:

> Immediate steps shall be taken for the purpose of bringing about an agreement with the Bristol & Exeter Railway Company for the joint use of the engine table belonging to that company at their Hendford station at Yeovil.
>
> Failing such arrangement and in the meantime we undertake on the part of the Salisbury & Yeovil Railway Company to make use of the triangle formed by the eastern and western forks and the mainline from Exeter to Salisbury as a means of turning the engines to be used on the line, and further no engine shall be run tender foremost. And we further undertake that an engine turntable shall be erected in or close to the joint station about to be built at Yeovil within three months from this date.

Both companies having made the above undertakings to the Board of Trade the opening of the line was allowed to proceed on Friday 1st June, 1860.

The *Western Flying Post* on 5th June reported the event in a low key under the heading 'Opening to Yeovil of the Salisbury and Yeovil Railway'.

> The opening for traffic of the last section of the above named railway - from Sherborne to Yeovil - took place on Friday last. There was no official demonstration, and the proceedings passed off in an entirely quiet manner. Beyond the influx of an unusual number of visitors (favoured by the delightful fineness of the weather) there was little to indicate that another branch had been opened of that great railway system of which Yeovil has become so important a centre.
>
> A streamer of flags was thrown across the street at the Choughs Hotel, and the Omnibuses decked themselves in laburnum. Numerous persons, who assembled at the railway stations for that purpose, witnessed the arrival and departure of trains in both towns and many

Advert for the opening of Salisbury & Yeovil Railway, *Western Flying Post*, 19th June, 1860.
Western Gazette

availed themselves of the opportunity of paying a first railway visit to their friends. The congratulations mutually exchanged will, we hope, prove a fitting commencement of the friendly intercourse of the two towns, now brought into such close communication.

The paper then gave a description of the newly-opened line,

The portion of the railway now opened leaving the Hendford station, which will temporarily be used by the South Western as well as the Bristol & Exeter company, passes for some distance along the branch line connecting the Hendford and Pen Mill stations. Diverging from thence it crosses by a splendid bridge the River Yeo. This bridge is an admirable piece of construction and may be regarded as one of the chief features in connection with the works. It consists of five arches, is 50 feet in span, and of cast iron. The line then joins the Wilts and Somerset, running parallel with it through a deep cutting. It then gradually rises, by an ascent of about one in 100, and crosses the Wilts and Somerset line near Clifton by a wrought iron bridge 50 ft long, and consisting of one arch. After joining the main line to Exeter, and passing through the cutting at Bradford Abbas, which from its depth was one of the most laborious and expensive parts of the undertaking, it runs close by Bradford village near the church, from the fine tower of which floated on this occasion a flag in honour of the day the only 'demonstration' of a public character that was anywhere visible. It then proceeds through nearly level country to Sherborne.

The gradients from Yeovil to the junction at Bradford are considerable, but after leaving that point become easy. The scenery presented on the newly opened line is of a great diversified and beautiful character. A lovely view of the grounds at Newton, the property of G. Harbin Esq. through which the railway takes a circuit, is presented, and near the point where the South Western and Wilts and Somerset lines meet one of the best views of the town, with the venerable tower of St Johns and the hills surrounding it is obtained. On emerging from the Bradford cutting a wide and splendid prospect places itself before the eye - an extensive and fertile valley on the bounds of which are seen the magnificent Park of the Earl of Ilchester at Melbury, and part of the equally magnificent and noble grounds surrounding Sherborne Castle. Indeed we scarcely know that any person desiring a short railway trip can select one more picturesque and attractive than that between Yeovil and Sherborne.

It is only necessary to add that the works have been carried on in the most expeditious and satisfactory manner, and energy truly indomitable has been displayed by the local manager, Mr Harrison, and the officials employed under him. The contractors, as our readers are aware, are the well know firm of Messrs Brassey & Co. We congratulate the town upon having become a terminus of another great and influential railway company, which will doubtless add to its traffic and importance.

The paper then went on to mention the works west of Yeovil,

Exeter and Yeovil Railway. This line which will complete the direct narrow gauge communication between Exeter and the metropolis is expected to be opened on the second of July. The contractor, Mr Taylor, has thrown every energy into the execution of the work in order to complete it as early as possible.

The assistant traffic manager of the LSWR, Mr Godson, had arrived on the previous day to superintend the opening arrangements. On the opening day various officials of the Salisbury & Yeovil company arrived in the town by the 12.33 pm train - including Mr Notman the Manager of the Salisbury & Yeovil company, Mr Townsend, Solicitor to the company, and Messrs G. Pain and R. Hetley of Salisbury, Directors. Following lunch with some of the officials involved in the construction of the line at the Three Choughs Hotel, they departed again at 3.30 pm.

The opening train service consisted of four up and five down trains, the first down train commencing from Salisbury. On Sundays there were two trains in each direction to and from London, which used the simple expedient of retaining the existing timetable over the earlier part of the line with the extra time between Sherborne and Yeovil added. The service allowed travel to London in 4 hrs 15 mins with a return journey of 4 hrs 33 mins by the fastest trains - although the 12.43 pm from Yeovil took 5 hrs 7 mins to reach Waterloo whilst the slowest down train was the 10.51 am arriving in Yeovil at 3.33 pm taking 4 hrs 42 mins. As both Pen Mill and the LSWR station were of almost equal distance from their respective London terminus, the timings on the GWR route were in some cases the same.

gauge was cheaper to construct and was accepted by the other railway companies, leaving the Great Western isolated as far as through traffic was concerned. As the minority party, to expand its traffic potential it had to conform to the majority. It was to be a long and expensive procedure on which work had commenced in 1863, and was to continue for 29 years.

By the summer of 1874 it was the turn of the former Wilts, Somerset and Weymouth lines to be converted. To enable the preliminary work to proceed sections of double line were operated as single line with a reduced train service on 16th, 17th and 18th June. Only three trains in each direction ran over the Westbury-Weymouth section, the up trains departing Yeovil at 9.30 am, 1.30 pm and 4.50 pm, and the down ones at 9.32 am, 4.47 pm and 8.22 pm.

At 11 pm on Thursday 18th June the last broad gauge engine left Weymouth. On board there was an inspector to check that all broad gauge stock had been cleared from the system, each station master *en route* furnishing a certificate to the effect that all broad gauge sidings under his control had been cleared. This engine left Yeovil Pen Mill at a little after midnight, bringing to an end the broad gauge era on the Wilts, Somerset & Weymouth line.

A considerable amount of preparatory work had been carried out, for some weeks previously men had been employed in clearing out the ballast to facilitate the movement of sleepers and rails and to saw partly through the transoms. Where the rails were laid on conventional chairs and sleepers, additional chairs were placed on the sleepers set at the new gauge, and all bolts and fittings freed ready for a swift change over.

To enable the work to be completed in as short a time as possible gangs of workmen were brought in from all over the GWR system. The line was divided into sections, each with two gangers in charge of 20 platelayers. Between Castle Cary and Dorchester there were 6 inspectors, 23 gangers, and 412 men (excluding the local gangs involved), engineers being based at Yeovil, Maiden Newton and Dorchester.

Work commenced at 2 am on the Friday morning and continued until dusk, the men sleeping in makeshift accommodation at the sites. The men had to bring provisions for three days, after which they could leave their workplace to obtain more food. The company provided a drink consisting mainly of oatmeal mixed with sugar called 'skilley', one man from each gang being deputed to brew this mixture and distribute it in large buckets into which individual workers dipped a tin cup.

Work had commenced on the 16th June when the down line of the double line sections was taken out of use and narrowed, the train service running over the up road under single line working with a pilotman. Conversion of the up lines and goods branches took place between 22nd and 26th June, Clifton Maybank being completed on the 25th.

Although much was achieved during that long weekend there remained more to be done over the next few weeks, and four months later there were reports of goods yards not yet returned to normal and delays to trains on the Wilts, Somerset & Weymouth line due to uncompleted station work! At Yeovil Pen Mill the station arrangements had been modified; the remains of the old down side train shed were removed and the island platform introduced to make easy cross-platform changes between trains.

A GWR pannier tank arrives at Clifton Maybank exchange sidings with a transfer goods from Yeovil Pen Mill during 1933. Although a daily occurrence, very few photographs have been taken of this working.   *Brunel University, Mowat Collection*

This view taken in August 1948 shows the Clifton Maybank transfer shed in its original form before the ends were 'bricked up'. Clearly shown are the differences between the two portals with the broad gauge to the left, and standard gauge to the right. Between the shed and the water tower the siding leads to the Yeovil Junction turntable with a 'King Arthur' class engine standing on the approach.   *D.B. Clayton*

The branch train connecting with the 5 pm Waterloo train departed 32 minutes late at 9.02 pm, and the second portion of the down 5 pm arrived at 9.19 pm and the branch train connecting with this departed at 9.36 pm. The signalman in Yeovil Junction East box set the points right for the branch train to start before lowering the signal, and in doing so he turned the disc signal working with the points at the trailing end of the crossover road leading onto the up main line into the all-right position. Upon seeing this and taking it as a signal for his train to shunt back the brakeman of the goods train signalled the driver to do so. As the branch train, consisting of Beattie standard well tank No. 252, two third class carriages, one second class, one first class and a brake van, approached the points leading onto the Yeovil Town branch, the driver saw the goods train backing towards him. Despite an application of the brakes there was a collision in which two wagons were derailed with much damage and the leading four wheels of the engine were also derailed. Fortunately, apart from being shaken up, neither the crew or any of the passengers received serious injury. Horse buses were quickly laid on to convey the passengers to Yeovil Town, and a breakdown gang summoned to clear the line which was completed by 5 am on the Sunday morning.

At the subsequent enquiry the brakeman of the goods train admitted that the accident was his fault and that he had no right to move the train without the orders of the shunter. However, Major Marindin, the Board of Trade inspector, accepted this but was critical of the signalling arrangements, stating that the disc signal should be worked by a separate lever and interlocked with the starting signal from the middle line with which it was a directly conflicting signal. And it should be a general rule that when a crossover road is signalled at both ends, the two signals should be worked by different levers and interlocked. The branch train was only braked by the steam brake on the engine and the 'Newalls' hand brake in the brake van, the Major commenting, '. . . if the train had been fitted throughout with a continuous brake the collision would have been less violent, even if it had not been entirely averted'.

During 1886 the daily service along the Durston branch consisted of six passenger trains each way daily - all terminating at Durston where passengers changed for Taunton and other destinations. Of the three goods trains that ran, one went to Weston-super-Mare, and one to Highbridge. On alternate Mondays a cattle train departed Taunton at 10.30 am running via Durston and Yeovil to Salisbury.

Further improvements to services took place on 3rd August, 1889 when the first boat train between Paddington and Weymouth Quay stopped at Yeovil. Two days later the first up boat train arrived in the town - a service that continued for 70 years except during the two World Wars.

The summer months brought much excursion traffic to the railways. It was the age of the annual factory outing where the employer treated his staff to a day out at a suitable location. On Saturday 16th May, 1891 almost 500 factory hands of Messrs Reymond & Son travelled to Plymouth by special train, and it was also noted that employees of Messrs Petter's also enjoyed an outing on the same day.

Contemporary reports of the period also give an insight into the workings of the period. One would have thought that the most expeditious route from Crewkerne to Weymouth was via Yeovil Junction, Yeovil Town and Yeovil Pen Mill, thence via the GWR line to Weymouth. However, when 580 employees of the West Somerset and Devon Manufacturing Company of Crewkerne made the trip by special train in July 1891 they travelled via Templecombe and the Somerset & Dorset Railway to gain access at Broadstone to the LSWR line to Weymouth, the return journey taking 2 hours 45 minutes!

On the evening of Tuesday 13th July, 1897 a further accident took place involving the Yeovil Town-Junction shuttle, this time self inflicted! '700' class 0-6-0 goods engine No. 690 had brought the branch train from Yeovil Town and stopped in the middle road at Yeovil Junction, whereupon the engine ran around the stock ready to depart at 6.47 pm. Unfortunately as the engine backed onto the train the driver was unable to close the regulator, and despite an application of both the vacuum and hand brakes, No. 690 struck the six-coach train at between 5 and 10 mph, driving the coaches back about 30-40 yards but they did not become derailed.

The first coach - the guard's van suffered very little damage, but the second vehicle - a third class coach - was severely damaged with broken windows, smashed doors and lamps dislodged from their sockets. The 10 passengers on board were thrown from their seats, nine receiving injuries - mainly bruising and cuts, but one suffering a broken arm.

Major Marindin, who carried out the Board of Trade investigation into the collision, concluded that the accident was not the driver's fault owing to the malfunction of the regulator. No. 690 was less than five months old at the time and 'jamming regulators' were one of the teething - troubles experienced with this class, there having been several other incidents!

The contents of the report did, however, give an insight into working methods at that time. The engine, being a six-wheel-coupled tender engine was not well suited to the working these branch trains, which should be - and usually were

> . . . worked with tank engines. Further than this, I do not think it is at all a good practice to take these main line engines on their arrival at Yeovil and put them in charge of a strange driver to work the branch trains until the time they are required to take the return train to London. Men always work better with an engine to which they are accustomed, and there ought to be sufficient engines at Yeovil to work the branch train with these proper drivers. [At that time 690 was a Salisbury-based engine and had no doubt worked a down goods to Yeovil before performing local duties.]

However, the saying that accidents happen in threes proved correct, for on Monday 26th July an empty coach being shunted onto a Waterloo train at Yeovil Junction became derailed blocking the up main and the branch for an hour, whilst on Thursday 27th foreman Delamont of the GWR goods department at Hendford was injured when two horses engaged in shunting forced him against a wagon.

Although the GWR operated two goods yards at Yeovil - Pen Mill and Hendford - there was still a lack of space and duplication of resources. During 1897 it was decided that Pen Mill would concentrate on mileage traffic whilst Hendford handled cartage traffic. This resulted in the reconstruction of Hendford goods shed and office, the contract being let on 5th September, 1899 to Messrs J.W & H. Child of Kingston Works, Yeovil for £2,887, thus bringing Yeovil's 19th century railway expansion to a close.

vehicles including a slip coach - was heading towards North box where Prosser had kept all his signals at danger. Approaching Pen Mill the line curves to the left to give the driver a poor view from a GWR locomotive which is driven from the right-hand side, and it is from that point that distances were subsequently disputed between driver and signalman at later inquiries. Upon approaching the down distant which was at caution, Dowler shut off steam and made a brake application. Signalman Prosser was watching his 'Track Occupied' indicator and waited 20 seconds before lowering his outer home signal, by which time the train had reduced speed to between six and eight miles per hour. Prosser then lowered the inner home signal when the train was about 20 yards from it, and it was therefore travelling at walking pace as it approached the North box starting signal which remained at 'Danger' to protect the excursion train which was still standing a short distance ahead.

Prosser saw the driver looking back at the signal box, and fearing that he was about to run by the starting signal he held up his hands to attract the driver's attention - but in vain! The engine passed the signal and crashed at low speed into the rear of the excursion. At the moment of impact the excursion train locomotive was shunting its two vehicles back onto the train.

No. 3710 buried itself into the rear coach, clerestory third No. 1902 being completely destroyed. The rear three compartments were crushed together, the sides bursting outwards as the roof rode over the locomotive and it was in this coach that the fatalities and serious injuries occurred. Rescue work was commenced immediately but it took a considerable time to extract the dead and injured owing to the compressed nature of the wreckage and the tools of the period available for rescue work. It was further hampered by the fact that the leading van of the express had derailed which prevented the locomotive from being moved back.

Despite the accident having occurred in such a cramped station, single line working was established over the up line between Marston Magna and Yeovil at 7.35 pm and normal two line working resumed at 2.52 am the following morning. Although the rear coach of the excursion was completely destroyed, and the second vehicle, brake third No. 2184, received considerable damage, the third carriage from the point of impact suffered only a broken top light, whereas all nine coaches of the express received damage - mainly to buffers and draw gear. Locomotive No. 3710 suffered a broken front vacuum pipe and the step under the smoke box, a trailing buffer and a leading bogie axle box were damaged, the front handrail was bent and the front of the footplate bent upwards.

Two passengers were killed instantly in the smash, Mrs Louise Redmond of Queens Park, Paddington, and Mrs Jane Legg of Bridport. A third, Miss May Groves of Evershot, died later of her injuries in Yeovil hospital. Her sister, Miss Emma Groves, was the most seriously injured and had both legs amputated. Six other passengers received serious injuries and about 40 were reported as having minor injuries and shock.

The inquest into the accident was held at Yeovil Town Hall, where driver Dowler stated that he always made a habit of looking at signal boxes as he passed them. He saw the signalman 'was motioning', but before he could make

The scene at Yeovil Pen Mill station on 8th August, 1913, taken not long after the collision. Rescuers are still freeing trapped passengers from the shattered remains of clerestory third No. 1902, the roof of which can be seen forced over the top of the locomotive No. 3710 *City of Bath*.
Author's Collection

A view taken later in the evening shows the almost complete destruction of the rear coach, although the collision was only at slow speed, it clearly demonstrating the frailty of wooden-bodied stock.   *Author's Collection*

out what was meant he had passed the starting signal. Fireman Richard Carver corroborated his driver's evidence concerning the sequence of the signals being 'pulled off' until they passed the inner home signal, where he saw the starting signal ahead at Danger. He also saw the signalman pointing in their direction, after which he attended to the engine, turning on the injector. When he returned to his side of the footplate (the left side) he saw the starting signal was still at danger. He shouted out, and heard the driver apply the brake as he screwed on the tender handbrake. Carver stated that they first discovered the train in front when they were about the length of an engine from it, and their speed was between three and four miles per hour.

The actions of the crew were open to question, for why would a driver look back at a signal box when entering a station whilst being brought in 'under caution', and the fireman turn on the injector at that precise moment? The latter operation could have done when the train had come to a stand! It was also odd that they had failed to see the train until they were about an engine's length from it - less than 80 ft - as it was a clear summer evening!

There was also much discussion and many questions concerning the actions of the station staff in the time leading up to the collision, particularly in leaving the rear coach off the platform (being non-corridor vehicles passengers were unable to walk forward to alight). The Coroner's jury were concerned over the order in which the movements of the excursion train were carried out, but had the excursion been drawn forward it would have fouled the down line and prevented the departure of the branch train which, although in the up platform, had to cross over to the down line to gain access to the branch.

Ironically there were passengers in the rear coach of the excursion who had wished to join the branch train but were unable to do so because they could not alight. Tragically Mrs Redmond was one. With hindsight it would have been safer to have drawn the excursion onto the branch until the express had departed, then shunted it back and removed the coach.

The jury returned a verdict of 'Death through misadventure', adding a rider to the effect that the accident was brought about by the failure of driver Dowler to observe the North signal box starting signal, and that such failure arose from a momentary distraction of attention and not from culpable negligence. Lt Col P.G. Von Donop, who subsequently held an investigation on behalf of the Board of Trade, stated in his report that in his opinion, while signalman Prosser did not quite carry out the signalling regulations on that occasion, the main responsibility for the accident rested with driver Dowler.

Col Van Donop added as a final remark:

Yeovil station is a comparatively old one, and its arrangements cannot be regarded as entirely satisfactory. The platforms have not sufficient length to completely accommodate the trains, and owing to the curvature of the lines, the driver of a down train does not obtain a good view of the line in front of him when he is entering the station. The company state that the question of remodelling this station has been for some time under consideration. It is, I consider, desirable that this should be taken in hand at an early date.

A GWR outside-framed pannier tank runs 'wrong road' through the up platform of Yeovil Pen Mill. Amongst the rolling stock in the sidings, a clerestory bogie coach, a four-wheeler and a six-wheeler. These vehicles were held as spares to strengthen both branch and main line trains if required.   *Author's Collection*

An un-named 'Bulldog' 4-4-0 stands in the down platform at Yeovil Pen Mill. Passengers mill around parcels and milk churns standing on the platform - all once part of the everyday scene. It was in this location on that fateful day in August 1913 that a train, also hauled by a 4-4-0, was struck in the rear by No. 3710 *City of Bath*.   *Author's Collection*

Thus ended the official enquiries. Dowler voluntarily resigned and applied for his pension, and the GWR settled all claims quickly. An extract from the Board meeting of 3rd October well illustrates the management of the time:

That a letter be addressed to Doctor Marsh expressing the company's thanks for the services of medical men and the hospital matron and nurses and that honoraria amounting to 150 guineas be voted to those concerned, Dr Marsh being consulted in regard to its apportionment.

That the out of pocket expenditure of the hospital (about £75) be re-imbursed and a donation of 100 guineas made to its funds. That a letter of thanks be sent to Colonel March, the President of the Yeovil branch of the Red Cross Society, for the valuable assistance rendered by several members of the society, and to Mr J. A. Ball who placed his motor car at the disposal of the company and that the Chief Constable of Somersetshire should be communicated with to express the company's appreciation of the services rendered by the police.

That the nine persons specified who rendered valuable assistance be seen by a representative of the company and verbally thanked and that gifts of money or kind be made to them, ranging from one to three guineas.

Although the GWR claimed to have considered the remodelling of the station for some time, apart from a new signal box in 1937 and the drastic alterations brought about by the singling of the main line in 1968 no significant work ever took place. The argument could well be that two World Wars, the decline of traffic in the years between them, and the general run down of the Beeching era has made any scheme unviable.

The second serious accident to take place at Yeovil Junction happened on 4th July, 1914 when the 10.25 am Exeter-Salisbury goods became divided near Sutton Bingham. Some 200 yds from Yeovil Junction West signal box the rear portion caught up with the front part before it could be diverted into the loop, and with the resulting collision several wagons struck the box causing the top part to be pushed off the base and partly pitched down the embankment. Fortunately, apart from a rather shaken signalman there were no other injuries, although 22 wagons suffered damage.

The summer months had for many years been the time when the Yeomanry (now known as the Territorial Army) went on manoeuvres to various parts of the country, and in those pre-motor vehicle days the troops with their kit and horses travelled by train. One such movement took place on Thursday 14th May, 1914 when the West Somerset Yeomanry travelled to Minehead, 16 troops and an officer having travelled by local train from Crewkerne to Yeovil Town where they joined a special for the remainder of the journey picking up detachments along the branch to Langport. The officer's horses were conveyed in horseboxes whilst horses of other ranks were carried in cattle trucks. The entire load consisted of one brake composite, two thirds, one van, three horseboxes, and 13 cattle wagons.

The summer of 1914 was to see the last of such manoeuvres - and peace and prosperity for many years. The assassination of the heir to the Austrian throne, Archduke Franz Ferdinand, by a Serbian nationalist in Sarajevo on 28th June set off an explosive situation across Europe which within weeks culminated in the declaration of war on Germany on 4th August.

Yeovil Junction West signal box, following the accident of 4th July, 1914. Struck by a runaway goods train, the wooden top of the structure has been knocked clean off its stone base and sent down the embankment. It could have been worse for the signalman: to the left is the steep drop into the roadway leading under the arch to Clifton Maybank transfer shed!
Leslie Brooke Collection

Immediately the railways were taken over by the Government under the 1871 Regulation of the Forces Act. The LSWR was well versed in the movement of troops having many service establishments and camps in its area, but the operating of troop specials and military goods traffic now took precedence over normal passenger services. In October 1914, 92 specials passed through Yeovil Junction conveying Canadian troops from Plymouth to camps on Salisbury Plain.

By September 1914 half a million men had joined Kitchener's volunteer army, thus causing staff shortages in many industries including the railways, and putting a great deal of pressure on the remaining staff. On 12th July, 1915 supernumerary porter Robert Slade, whilst engaged in transferring goods loaded on a trolley from the up platform to the transfer shed by means of the boarded crossing at the west end of Yeovil Junction station, was knocked down and killed by a shunting engine travelling on the down local line, the driver's vision having been obstructed by wagons occupying the through roads. At the inquest the coroner's jury returned a verdict of accidental death, but made a suggestion that, whenever possible, shunting operations should cease whilst goods were being transferred over the crossing. However, the Traffic Committee responded that the proposal 'is one that cannot be adopted without causing serious delay'. A company inquiry into the circumstances reported that, 'had the engine whistle been sounded as a warning when the engine was approaching the crossing, the occurrence might have been avoided', and they were of the opinion 'that the unfortunate man met his death by omitting to exercise proper care when crossing the line'.

Three months later a second fatality took place at the same place. On 10th October, whilst 15 wagons were being shunted from the down local line at the west end of the station, shunter James Trimby - who was standing on the ramp of the down platform - attempted to apply the brake to the fifth wagon as it passed him. In doing so he slipped between the ramp of the platform and the wagons, sustaining severe injuries to his leg as a result of which he died in Yeovil Hospital on 23rd December. The resulting company inquiry again showed little sympathy: 'We are of the opinion the injury which the unfortunate man received resulted from his slipping on the coping stone of the platform ramp, and the occurrence must be considered as purely accidental'.

Although its resources were stretched with the vast amount of extra traffic, the LSWR summer timetable of 1915 still showed the five principal expresses to the West of England, but the popular 11 am from Waterloo ceased to have the various relief trains it had had in the past. Heavily loaded, often double heading was required and although timekeeping suffered, the booked allowance of 3 hours 18 minutes was maintained until 1918 when it was extended to 3 hours 57 minutes, and booked connections for North Devon and North Cornwall ceased with the introduction of the summer service. It was, however, still possible to dine in restaurant cars on some West of England trains.

On the GWR there were also changes to suit the war situation and there was a re-arrangement of the operating Divisions from the 1st January, 1915 when an additional division was formed with headquarters at Westbury to cover the main line from Enborne Junction (exclusive) to Athelney, the Westbury-Salisbury line, Castle Cary to Weymouth and the Portland branch, the Abbotsbury and Bridport branches, and the branch between Yeovil and Curry Rivel Junction.

Services on the Wilts, Somerset & Weymouth line were reduced, and no longer did the boat train run from Paddington to Weymouth for the Channel Island boats, as the sailings had been drastically reduced and at times ceased. Freight traffic increased with coal for the Royal Navy at Portland, supplies to other service establishments in the area and troop specials. The Petter's factory involvement in the war effort provided both an inwards trade in materials and the finished products outward. Yeovil had always been an important junction for servicemen travelling between various establishments, and the war vastly increased the numbers travelling. Shortage of staff and materials and the vast amounts of war traffic resulted in the Government during January 1917 sanctioning a fare increase of 50 per cent to dissuade travel. Many trains were taken off and a 60 mph speed limit was imposed, all of which did little to ease the situation. Further reductions were made locally in the summer of 1918 when the Joint Committee decided to withdraw the cartage service to Stoke and South Petherton during the period of Government control, whilst on the motive power side the 48 ft turntable situated at Yeovil Town Shed had been removed during 1917.

There was also the problem of the rapidly rising operating costs of the railways during the war period, and ways of cutting costs were high on the agenda of the Traffic Committee. In February 1918 it was suggested that improved lighting could be obtained in Yeovil Town parcel office by the provision of two skylights at a cost of £37, it being estimated that there would be a saving of 15,000 cubic feet of gas per annum! The LSWR was also at that time actively installing barriers at stations and introducing the use of platform tickets. At Yeovil Town some slight structural alterations costing £55 were necessary, and using a ticket machine already in stock it was estimated that 25s. a week could be raised from the sale of platform tickets (at a 1d. each)!

The slack working of a signalman at Yeovil Junction East box came to light on the 20th August, 1918. In order to free the Sykes treadle the signalman had allowed 'T9' class locomotive No. 730 to stand on the up branch line, but owing to his failure to place a lever collar over the levers protecting the engine he overlooked its presence. There was a mist and ground fog lying around and at 10.53 pm two engines coupled together proceeding from Yeovil Junction to Yeovil Town collided with No. 730 about 125 yards east of the signal box.

It was found that the signalman also allowed the key of the Sykes electric lock connected to the branch starting signal to remain in the instrument, and admitted that he was in the habit of so leaving it. On that occasion the Sykes key was also in the main line instrument and may have had some effect on the electric batteries. The practice of leaving the key in Sykes instruments was contrary to the regulations for signalling, and the signalman was transferred to a less important box and his bonus was forfeited for three months.

A further incident took place at Yeovil Junction on 5th June, 1922 at 3.45 pm. When 'L11' class 4-4-0 No. 440 was running tender first from the up bay platform into the dead-end siding it came into violent collision with the buffer stops, forcing them back and causing the parapet wall of the nearby bridge to be demolished. The tender was completely derailed and lifting gear had to be summoned from Yeovil shed to rerail the tender, this being completed at 8 pm.

The return of peace saw little improvement in train services as labour problems replaced those caused by war and the eight-hour working day came into force on 1st February, 1919. The one bright spot during that year was that the GWR recommenced the operation of Sunday school excursions.

The LSWR as with other railways, was short of motive power following the war and accepted the loan of 17 ROD 2-8-0 goods locomotives - a design based on the Great Central Railway's '8K' class heavy mineral engines designed by Robinson. Following a visit to Eastleigh works certain members of the class were allocated to Nine Elms, Strawberry Hill and Exmouth Junction to work main line goods duties. In January 1920 No. 2121 was noted to be regularly working the 12.25 am Nine Elms-Yeovil Junction goods, whilst Nos. 2122, 2123, and 2124 were working between Exmouth Junction and Salisbury. On 15th February, 1920 No. 2119 was reported working the 9.10 am Exeter-Templecombe stopping train. It is thought that this was the only occasion one of these 2-8-0s worked an LSWR passenger train! However, they were not totally suitable for the LSWR, the class were in store by the July and disposed of to other companies.

Although the war was over Government control of the railways remained until 15th August, 1921, shortly after the Railways Act proceeding through Parliament came into force. From the 1st January, 1923 the railway companies were grouped into what became known as 'The Big Four', the LSWR becoming part of the new Southern Railway (SR), whereas the Great Western was least affected by the upheaval and retained its old name and identity.

Chapter Nine

The Grouping Years

The world had changed from that of August 1914, and the railways no longer enjoyed their pre-war monopoly. The development of the motor lorry, the bus - and later the coach - were quickly to challenge them and alter the railway's place in society. This, together with wage rises, and industrial unrest both within and outside the industry, was to sweep away many of the previous practices and much of the rivalry between the companies as they struggled to come to terms with the changing world.

The death following illness of Frederick Dunsford, the popular Pen Mill station master, on 3rd March, 1926 was a bad start for a year in which the railways were to become embroiled in the General Strike. The actual strike commenced at midnight on Monday 3rd May, and although throughout the country few trains were running, it was reported that on the Tuesday and Thursday two trains had reached Paddington from Weymouth conveying Channel Island boat passengers, and a few trains also ran between Westbury and Weymouth, and on the Thursday the 4.30 pm Paddington-Weymouth had also run. On Friday the Westbury-Weymouth service operated, as did a train of milk empties from Paddington to Weymouth.

It appears that in the Yeovil area the strike had total support, the *Western Gazette* reporting that on Monday 10th the first two trains on the branch from Yeovil Town to Yeovil Junction ran with a volunteer driver, but on Wednesday 12th one of the regular drivers returned and three branch trains connected with up trains, the fireman being a volunteer. It was also reported that about eight trucks of coal which had been in the sidings since the beginning of the strike had been unloaded.

On Tuesday 11th Messrs Petter's had offered their shunting locomotive to the GWR to shunt Hendford goods yard, an offer they were considering when on the following day (Wednesday 12th) the strike was called off at noon. However, the return to normal took some time, as the railway companies took back strikers only as required - a situation that caused much resentment. The *Western Gazette* reported that on Thursday 13th there had been a marked improvement on the Weymouth line, although the railwaymen were still out and it was understood that they were awaiting instructions from the headquarters of their union. In fact on that day a service of four trains between Westbury and Weymouth and five return workings took place, whilst one train in each direction operated over the Durston branch. By Monday 17th this had been increased to four between Taunton and Yeovil and three between Yeovil and Taunton, whilst seven down trains ran from Westbury to Weymouth and eight in the up direction.

Despite the slow return to normal, on Whit Sunday 23rd May 250 passengers departed from Pen Mill for Weymouth on a half-day excursion and the following day 1,000 passengers departed in two trains for Weymouth on a day excursion. It was also reported that char-a-bancs were filled to capacity! It was a turning point for the railways as people had managed to travel during the

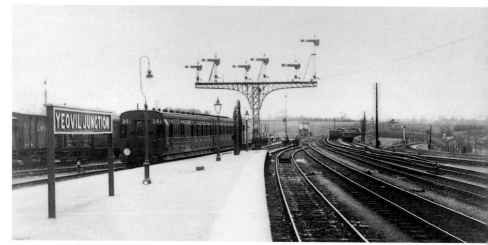

The signal gantry at the end of the up platform dominates the scene as auto-set No. 351 is propelled into the branch bay at Yeovil Junction by an 'O2' class 0-4-4T. To the extreme right the single track of the Clifton Maybank spur can be seen curving down to pass under the LSWR main line.   *R.C. Riley Collection*

'Dean Goods' No. 2543 approaches Yeovil Town from Pen Mill with a Taunton train on 2nd August, 1928. Wyndham Hill rises to the left as the track snakes its way between the two stations. No. 2543 was built in August 1897 and not withdrawn until February 1953, one of a class of engine that because of their simplicity and reliability served the GWR for many years and gave valuable service to the War Department in two World Wars.   *H.C. Casserley*

strike. Many local and rural bus services were already established and the motor lorry had also proved itself. Some traders continued to use road transport and much valuable traffic was lost to the railways forever.

On the morning of 25th June, 1926 fire destroyed the upper part of Hendford signal box. This was caused by the signalman attempting to melt some tar in a tin on the gas ring. Whilst this was taking place he left the signal box to visit the toilet, at which point the building went up in smoke. Following his interview with the divisional superintendent the signalman received the following memo, which ended:

> It is stated by your Inspector that you have been generally attentive to your duty (excepting of course during the period from 4th May to 15th when you were on strike) and in view of this it is decided not to entirely dispose of your services but a position of porter will be found for you on the understanding that in future you will pay proper attention and take care in connection with the performance of your duty.

The LSWR never had been a railway with named trains, but following the formation of the Southern Railway it was decided to name some of the principal expresses from Waterloo to the West Country; a competition was held amongst the staff for the most suitable names. In the event only the 11 am departure was named, the winner being 'The Atlantic Coast Express', the first run taking place on 19th July, 1926. It was an unusual titled train as it was not a new service, during the summer it ran in two parts, and four parts on Saturdays, and there was nothing 'Express' about the final parts of the journey. Its most novel claim to fame was the fact that as it proceeded westwards it split to serve 10 destinations, the train containing many brake composite coaches to allow this operation. Only one destination (Padstow) could truly claim to be on the Atlantic coast, whilst Sidmouth and Exmouth were moving the description into the realms of fantasy. However, the 'Atlantic Coast Express', or the 'ACE' as it was known, was special.

The workings were complex and varied over the years. The second part stopped at Yeovil Junction at 1.41 pm where the Sidmouth and Exmouth coaches were detached and placed on the rear of a following stopping train and again detached at Sidmouth Junction, likewise the up working was carried out by the same method at 12.54 pm. The introduction of the winter timetable on 20th September, 1926 saw the Yeovil Junction stop removed, the down and up trains stopping at Sidmouth Junction. The 1928 winter timetable saw the Sidmouth and Exmouth coaches detached and attached at Salisbury, from which time the 'ACE' was 'fast' through Yeovil Junction.

The repercussions of the General Strike were to have a lasting effect on the railways - particularly with the continued coal strike which seriously depleted a major source of revenue, added to which the loss of traffic to the up-and-coming road transport industry was beginning to have an effect. Although during 1926 it was recorded that more milk was forwarded through Yeovil, Yetminster and Evershot, the threat from the road was ever present. At Frome Messrs Vinter & Long had commenced to use Scammell tankers for the long distance conveyance of milk from their dairy, and were actively persuading others to follow. It was the first major sign of the railways losing a regular and valuable traffic, although in his annual report the divisional superintendent was confident:

The trade in Yeovil in the early part of the year was brisk, a considerable quantity of building being undertaken. Approximately 1,000 consignments of Sugar Beet seed were dealt with in the spring. Except for the actual period of the General Strike very little difference has been apparent in Yeovil. Coal traffic has been quiet, but in the last few weeks of the year has been particularly heavy. There has been a particularly heavy traffic in Sugar Beet during the last three months of the year, the traffic being dispatched to Ipswich. The building trade has been busy and many municipal houses are being erected.

Messrs Petters Ltd are working full time, and their engines are being dispatched in increasing quantities. The outlook in all branches is very favourable and a busy period is expected.

Despite this optimism, economies were being made. The joint passenger and goods receiving office in Wine Street, Yeovil, closed on 24th June, 1926, and Yeovil Town - like other many stations at the time - was causing concern to the Joint Officers Committee. In November 1923 the annual wage bill for the station joint staff was £3,565 16s. for the 22 staff. Ten years earlier the wage bill for 24 staff had been £1,606 12s., the increase in costs being due to wage rises and additional men to cater for the eight-hour working day, although the waiting room attendant had been withdrawn and three signalmen were saved in October 1916 with the opening of the new signal box.

Having scrutinised the duties of all staff there was little that could be done to make further economies until November 1933 when the co-ordination of goods supervisory arrangements at the Yeovil stations was introduced. During 1935 the possibility of concentrating and combining the collected and delivered goods traffic at one or other of the goods sheds was reviewed, only to reveal the inadequacies of both Yeovil Town and Hendford goods sheds.

The daily average number of goods wagons handled inwards and outwards for that type of traffic was GWR 20 inwards, 13 outwards and SR 15 inwards, 10 outwards, giving a total of 58 wagons. The problem was that Yeovil Town goods shed could accommodate only five wagons at a time, and owing to the awkward yard track layout most of the wagons for the coal and mileage sidings had to pass through the goods shed to gain access to the wagon turntables. Hendford goods shed could berth just six wagons under cover and the siding accommodation outside the shed was very limited, making it impossible to deal with the combined traffic at Hendford without considerable extension to the accommodation, whilst the situation at Yeovil Pen Mill was no better. It was therefore decided to allow the existing arrangements to continue. However, the decision of the Southern Railway to acquire Messrs Chaplin & Co., its cartage contractors, allowed the committee to look into the question of joint cartage.

Whilst these economies were being investigated some improvements were made to the stations at Yeovil Town and Pen Mill. Towards the end of 1930 approval was given for the provision of a new parcel office and gents toilet at Yeovil Town at an estimated cost of £2,830. To utilise the booking office staff more efficiently a 'passimeter' type booking office was authorised in October 1932, and in January 1933 authorisation was given to convert Pen Mill similarly at a cost of £244.

During early 1934 the vast overall roof was removed from Yeovil Town station, the cost of the replacement canopies being £3,400 - although it was quickly pointed out at the Joint Committee meeting that the coverage of the area used by the GWR had been reduced from 260 ft to 170 ft! The station was also equipped with electric light at a cost of £250, it being estimated that this would bring an annual saving of £32. The Brunel overall roof of Pen Mill was also removed, but again canopies had to be constructed and a covering provided for the footbridge that had previously been under the overall roof.

A visit by the Southern Railway General Manager to Yeovil Town during 1935 could well have changed the course of history had his ideas been carried out. Unimpressed by the cramped location of the shed, and more importantly the number of light engine movements to and from Yeovil Junction and along the main line, a site for a new shed at Templecombe was investigated. However, the cost of construction and the problems of accommodation for over 100 men and their families in a place that was little more than a village added to the difficulties and the matter was allowed to drop.

The rapid expansion of both urban and rural bus services was to give the railways much cause for concern, extra halts being constructed in an attempt to stem the loss of trade. The first to open in the Yeovil area was on 28th November, 1927 at Thorney & Kingsbury, on the Durston branch west of Martock. Situated beneath an overbridge, it served both the nearby villages. A second halt on the branch was opened at Hendford on Monday 2nd May, 1932. This was constructed on the north side of the line opposite the signal box and consisted of a 145 ft long timber platform supported on trestles. At the time the site was quite rural, for Yeovil had failed to expand much in that direction except for the nearby Westland's Factory whose employees were the principal customers. The fare from Pen Mill or Town stations was 2½d. single, 3d. return. The structure was not inspected until 13th May, 1933 when in his report the inspector noted that about 150 passengers a month used the facility. However official figures for tickets sold and revenue received were 2,233 raising £204 in 1933, rising to a peak of 2,976 for £342 in 1936, but by 1938 this had fallen to 2,341 persons travelling to give an income of £313, suggesting that local bus services again had begun to abstract local traffic. Soon after this the war situation was to distort the figures as Westland's went into full war production.

The GWR next turned its attention to the main line between Yeovil and Dorchester along which four halts were opened between 1931 and 1936; Bradford Peverell & Stratton, Cattistock, Chetnole, and Thornford Bridge. The latter, which opened on 23rd March, 1936, was situated three miles south of Yeovil. With the halts came an improved auto-train service between Weymouth and Yeovil, this being further enhanced on 17th February, 1936 when two diesel railcars were introduced onto the Bristol-Weymouth service. In the early days one return working from Weymouth terminated at Yeovil Pen Mill, from where a return journey was made over the Durston branch. This ran non-stop between Yeovil Town and Taunton (except for the exchange of train staff at crossing stations), the 'express' working taking 20 minutes off the timings of the conventional branch train. Upon return to Yeovil the railcar continued to Trowbridge and Bristol Temple Meads as a semi-fast service.

When introduced the railcars were reputed to be operating the fastest such service in the country at that period, considering the gradients over the Wilts,

With a scream on the whistle and framed by the station footbridge, 'King Arthur' class No. 746 *Pendragon* races through Yeovil Junction with the up 'Atlantic Coast Express' on 21st May, 1935.
H.C. Casserley

One of Yeovil's long lasting 'U' class moguls, No. 1792 waits to depart from Yeovil Junction with the 11.16 am Exeter Central-Salisbury on 21st May, 1935. In the background (in the up sidings) is a private owner coal wagon belonging to Bradford's, a company, which has served Yeovil for 150 years. Built in May 1925 as a 2-6-4 tank No 792 *River Arun*, and running only 69,994 miles, she was rebuilt as a tender engine in July 1928 and withdrawn in September 1964.   *H.C. Casserley*

Somerset & Weymouth section. The 12.7 miles from Yeovil Pen Mill to Maiden Newton was covered in 16 minutes, which included the 2¼ mile climb of 1 in 52 towards Evershot tunnel. The 10.10 am service from Weymouth covered the Castle Cary-Westbury section in 18 minutes - a distance of 19.6 miles.

Excursion traffic was not neglected during this period, the ever-popular half-day summer excursions to Weymouth run from Pen Mill always attracting good loads. On 10th June, 1934, 261 passengers travelled whilst on 26th August some 469 departed from Pen Mill at 1.10 pm. An excursion from Yeovil to Porthcawl on 5th August is reported to have picked up 403 passengers *en route*.

Sunday School outings were still generating good revenue at the time. On 28th June over 800 travelled from Pen Mill to Weymouth, 250 children and 50 parents from the Baptist Sunday Schools departing at 8.50 am, whilst another train containing 120 children and 80 parents from the Salvation Army and 250 from the Pen Mill Methodist Sunday School also travelled to Weymouth. On the same date 130 members of South Street Sunday School visited the resort in a fleet of five motor coaches. The choice of travel had become easier! Three years later the figures for half-day excursions were higher, 707, 270, 300 and 392 passengers for the four Sundays in August.

Great efforts were made to explore the potential of excursion traffic, not only in complete trains but also by allowing booking facilities on existing services and the use of excursions commencing at other stations along the line. The *Western Gazette* for 14th September, 1934 carried the following announcement:

A number of excursions from Yeovil and Sherborne have been announced by the Southern Railway. On Sunday September 16th from Yeovil Town and Junction there is a trip to North Devon and Cornwall, while on the same day there is also excursions to a number of places in Devonshire, Salisbury, Chichester, Worthing, Hove and Brighton from Yeovil Town and Junction, and on Wednesday September 19th from Yeovil Town and Junction and Sherborne a trip is being run to London and Windsor.

As previously stated, the railways were losing milk traffic to the roads - a decline that had commenced during the 1920s. The railways took up the challenge, but it was clear that they would have to use bulk tanks instead of the many churns which took up a vast amount of space and were time consuming to handle, although the churn took many years to disappear entirely from the railway scene.

On the Salisbury-Exeter line, Yeovil had since the earliest days been a centre for milk train operations, inasmuch as milk trains commenced or terminated there, and the large creamery and cheese factory of Messrs Aplin & Barrett situated near to Yeovil Town station generated a considerable amount of trade. However, a report on the latter company's progress in October 1933 stated that as well as factories in London, Westbury and Frome, there were 32 distribution depots up and down the country. There were through parcel vans operating on the railway system and over 100 motor vehicles to aid distribution, and it was clear that the railways were already losing a large amount of local traffic from this one Yeovil factory.

During 1931 the Southern Railway had opened sidings serving dairies on its system in the West Country, those nearest to Yeovil being at Seaton Junction and Chard Junction, whilst an existing siding served Semley. Sherborne

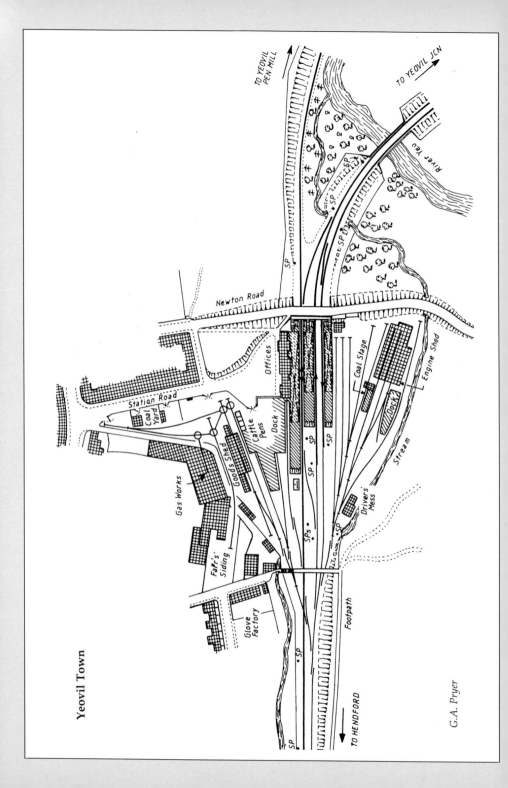

Yeovil Town

TO YEOVIL PEN MILL

TO YEOVIL JCN

River Yeo

SP

SP

SP

SP

Newton Road

Offices

Station Road

Coal Yard

Cattle Pens

Gas Works

Goods Shed

Dock

SP

SP

SP

Coal Stage

Dock

Engine Shed

Stream

Drivers Mess

SP

SP

Farr's Siding

Glove Factory

Footpath

SP

SP

TO HENDFORD

G.A. Pryer

Yeovil Pen Mill

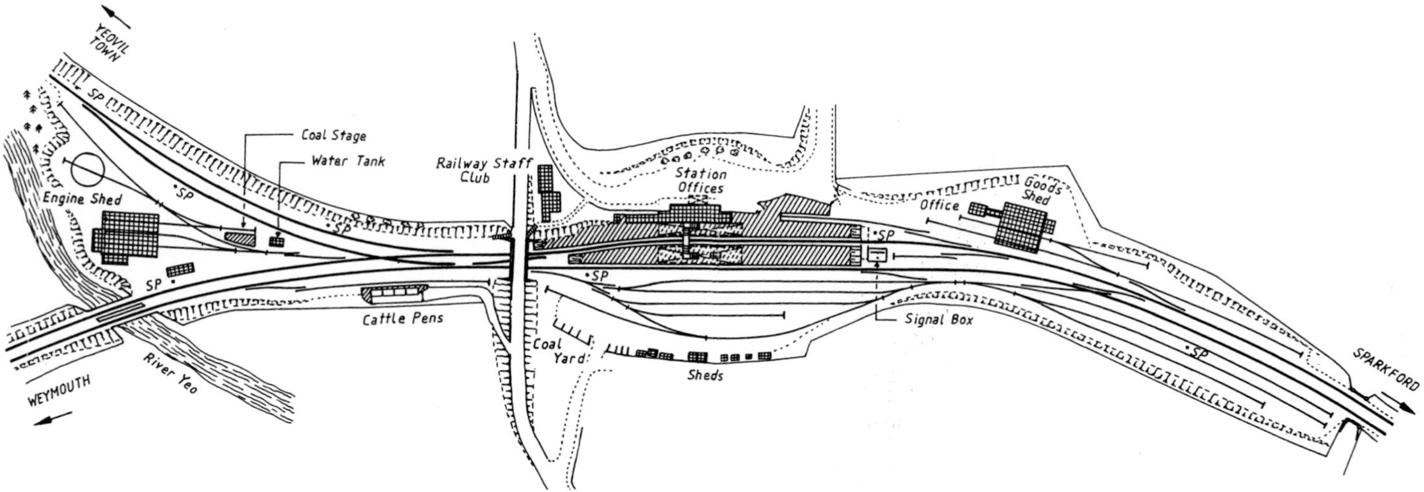

G.A. Pryer

SPARKFORD

SP

Signal Box

Goods Shed

Office

Station Offices

9.0 p.m.

SP

Coal Yard

Sheds

SP

Railway Staff Club

Cattle Pens

Coal Stage

Water Tank

SP

SP

SP

YEOVIL TOWN

Engine Shed

SP

River Yeo

WEYMOUTH

Yeovil Town uncovered! Photographed in March 1934 a view of Yeovil Town station during the brief period shortly after the removal of the overall train shed and before the new platform canopies had been erected. To the left is the goods shed and in the far background the chimneys of Aplin & Barrett's creameries, an important customer to the railways for the distribution of their products.   *Brunel University Mowat Collection*

The Tudor-style of architecture at Yeovil Town shows up clearly in this pre-nationalisation view of the exterior of the station, a building the *Western Gazette* described at the time of its construction as 'The most impressive commercial building in the town'. The board 'Southern & Great Western Railways' extols the station's joint ownership, whilst above in the gable end a carved stone '1860' commemorates the building date albeit a year early!   *Author's Collection*

handled a considerable amount of churn traffic, and traffic from the Somerset & Dorset was transferred at Templecombe.

The GWR also took up the challenge. On the Weymouth line during the 1920s an up milk train departed Weymouth at 4.21 pm calling at Maiden Newton, Yetminster, and Yeovil to pick up 'Siphon' vans loaded with churns, some of those at Yeovil having arrived off the Durston branch, further churns being collected at Marston Magna, Sparkford and Castle Cary.

During 1931 the GWR approved the provision of private sidings at Sparkford for the Sparkford Vale Co-op Dairy Society, and for United Dairies at Yetminster, and in April 1932 at Thorney & Kingsbury for the Nestles & Anglo Swiss Condensed Milk Company.

On 26th January, 1933 the first road-rail milk tanks departed from Maiden Newton, whilst milk tanks were introduced at other locations in conjunction with private sidings, but a huge amount of churn traffic remained. It was reported that during 1939 the Southern Railway dispatched a total of 9,300,000 gallons of milk from Seaton Junction, Chard Junction, Sherborne and Semley, the railways having negotiated hard to save losing more traffic to the roads.

Indeed it was not only milk that was being lost, agricultural traffic in general being in decline as the improved motor lorries and the services they provided demonstrated greater flexibility. In 1936 a special committee was set up to investigate the means of retaining and regaining trade. It was to be difficult. The transportation of grain and cattle cake to farms in the Yeovil area was investigated, it emerging that during that year Yeovil handled 7,700 tons, Martock 3,000 tons, Montacute 300 tons, Marston Magna 450 tons and Sparkford 650 tons, although at the latter 2,095 tons had been brought into the district directly by road haulage mainly from Bristol.

A joint report by both companies into livestock traffic at Yeovil Market concluded that in serving an area of approximately 15 miles radius many of the places were remote from stations and rail transport in such cases between the farm and Yeovil market was impracticable, although the position with regard to long distance traffic from the market was extremely favourable, there being little or no road competition. The question of both companies jointly providing additional road vehicles at Yeovil to operate in competition with the road haulers could not be justified bearing in mind that practically all the long distance traffic was already sent by rail. Again there were further losses of milk traffic during 1938 to road transport, especially from Sparkford and Castle Cary.

For several years attention had been focused on the Clifton Maybank spur. Although a good number of wagons were transferred there between the GWR and SR, on average there being three trips each way daily from Yeovil Pen Mill, there would be little difficulty in that traffic being routed via Yeovil Town to Yeovil Junction. Since the abandonment of the broad gauge in 1874 the main purpose of the transfer shed had become academic, and it was decided the small amount of wagon load traffic transferred there by Yeovil Junction staff could be undertaken at Yeovil Junction station platform instead of the transfer shed.

The scheme would save both manpower and maintenance charges, the Clifton Maybank branch could be lifted and Clifton Maybank Junction signal box closed saving two class '5' signalman at £260 pa, annual maintenance costs

Hendford

General arrangement drawing of Hendford and associated sidings.

G.A. Pryer

of £261, plus an estimated expenditure of £220 on reconditioning a small bridge; there was also the locomotive mileage to be saved. The only problem was that Mr Wyatt Paul, Lord of the Manor of nearby Bradford Abbas who also ran three farms in the area, had a private siding running off the branch half way along its length. Mr Paul entered into an agreement whereby he would use alternative facilities consisting of a section of line contiguous with the Clifton Maybank old goods platform and the platform itself, and that a cart track from the platform to the entrance to his land be provided and maintained by the GWR. Thus on 7th June, 1937 the Clifton Maybank branch closed, with Clifton Maybank Junction signal box closing on 1st November. During the same year the private siding into Bunford Flax Mill, situated on the south side of the Durston branch between Westland's siding and Watercombe Lane overbridge, was also taken out of use. With these changes the gradual erosion of goods traffic and the reduction of facilities was halted as war clouds gathered over Europe.

Throughout the summer of 1939 the international situation deteriorated, although many were taking their holidays as usual and timetables had been published for the forthcoming winter. However, the railways - like many other organisations - had been planning and preparing for the inevitable for several years and were quick to put their plans into action, the Government taking over the main line companies under the Emergency Powers (Defence) Act on 1st September, war being declared on Sunday 3rd September, 1939. The previously advertised cheap day excursion to Exeter and Exmouth that was to have run that day was cancelled, and as with many towns in the West Country, Yeovil and the surrounding district became the home to evacuees. The first two trains conveying them arrived at Yeovil Town station on Friday 1st September followed by two on the Saturday and a further three on Sunday, buses taking those billeted to outlaying districts from the reception centres. Finally a total of 11,000 child and adult evacuees was billeted in the district, 4,400 within the Borough.

Services were reduced and an overall speed limit of 60 mph was imposed. All GWR West of England expresses were diverted via Bristol, thus reducing the connections available for passengers over the Westbury-Yeovil-Weymouth section. At the same time seat reservations, slip coaches, and restaurant car facilities were withdrawn, although the latter were restored on both the GWR and SR on 16th October.

The imposition of the blackout and lack of lighting in general - including the use of blue lamps and drawn blinds during the hours of darkness - added to the misery of travel in the early days of the war. The emergency timetables that had been brought into force were revised from 25th September and during December the speed limit was raised to from 60 to 75 mph, West of England expresses reverting to travel via Westbury and the Langport cut-off.

Exceptionally cold weather during early 1940 did nothing to ease travel conditions. The requisitioning by the War Department of some of the GWR 0-6-0 'Dean Goods' locomotives resulted in engines from other companies being loaned to cover the shortage. By January 1940 two LMS '3F' 0-6-0s, Nos. 3543 and 3689, were to be seen at Yeovil whilst working the daily Westbury-Weymouth goods.

On 7th February, 1940 King George VI visited the Westland aircraft factory and other places in the area, the Royal Train consisting of 11 coaches hauled by

'Castle' class 4-6-0 No. 5069 *Isambard Kingdom Brunel*, arriving at Pen Mill at 1.50 am and proceeding onto the single line towards Yeovil Town where it was stabled for the remainder of the night. It was hauled back into Pen Mill at 9.25 am to allow the King to alight before the stock proceeded to Weymouth for servicing, returning to Pen Mill at 4.15 pm before going on to Yatton where it was stabled for the following night.

The time of the invasion scare saw the construction of pill boxes at strategic points to defend the railways - then seen as the vital transport network - and many of these became the responsibility of various Home Guard units. Added to these the railways had formed their own units, the principal one in the area being the 22nd Devon (5th Southern Railway) Battalion. There were Somerset railwaymen in both 'A' and 'B' companies drawn from staff between Chard Junction and Yeovil stations. 'A' Company headquarters was at Yeovil Town station and 'E' Company at Templecombe, Somerset & Dorset men also belonging to that unit.

The presence of Westland's aircraft factory, the military camps at Lufton and Houndstone and the nearby airfield at Yeovilton, plus the fact that Yeovil was an important junction in the railway system, made the town vulnerable to air attack, and during the conflict 95 buildings were destroyed and no less than 1,246 damaged in air raids.

The first test of strength came on Monday 30th September, 1940 when a formation of 50 German bombers was intercepted by fighters over Yeovil. Within minutes they had turned east to drop 300 bombs on Sherborne killing 17 and injuring 32. The war had spread to rural England! Minor disruption was caused on 9th May, 1941 when a German bomber caught a balloon cable near Yeovil, resulting in the aircraft jettisoning two bombs which failed to explode after landing near the Durston branch at Yew Tree Close Farm.

By September 1941 the first two Bulleid 'Merchant Navy' class pacifics 21C1 (35001) and 21C2 (35002) were to be seen at Yeovil Junction working Salisbury - Exmouth Junction goods trains, whilst at Pen Mill as well as the LMS '3Fs', LNER 'O1/4' 2-8-0 and LMS '8F' 2-8-0 engines were appearing on Westbury-Weymouth freights. The Bulleid pacific's increased; following modifications 21C3 (35003) was by May running though Yeovil Junction non-stop with 15-coach test trains between Salisbury and Exeter. By August the pacifics were working regular passenger services, and No. 21C10 (35010) worked a 20-coach test train to Exeter on 2nd December. On the Westbury-Weymouth line early 1942 saw the introduction of one of the two GWR twin-set diesel railcars working certain Bristol-Weymouth services, although its stay was short lived.

The most serious raid to affect the railway in the Yeovil area took place on Thursday 3rd September, 1942. '1854' class 0-6-0 pannier tank No. 1729 had departed from Yeovil Shed earlier in the morning and, having banked a freight train up Brewham Bank, returned to Castle Cary where the crew were relieved by another Yeovil crew who had travelled up on a passenger train.

Driver Jack Shergold and fireman Tom Whittle had just taken over and moved along the down line in preparation to shunt wagons to form the local goods to Durston, when at 9.15 am a lone Junkers 88 swept in low from the Yeovil direction and dropped four 500 kg bombs. The first one completely destroyed No. 1729, killing driver Shergold, seriously injuring fireman Whittle and wrecking eight wagons. The second destroyed the signal box, killing the signalman and also demolishing the goods shed and parcel office, whilst the third destroyed the Railway Hotel and caused damage to Prideaux's dairy and three cottages. The fourth bomb landing in the river.

Castle Cary was an important junction and there was a swift response to repairs, by 11 pm the same day traffic was again passing towards Yeovil - albeit over a single line controlled by hand signals. Two days later a temporary 22-lever wooden signal box came into use, whilst a brick built 85-lever box of ARP design opened on 27th October.

The risk of an air raid causing severe damage amongst engines at Yeovil Town shed was minimised by stabling a number of them at Yeovil Junction during the threat of heavy air raids. Fortunately the effectiveness of this preventive measure was never put to the test.

At the same time the need for Southern Railway engine crews to know an alternative route in the event of their own line being closed by bombing was met in the Autumn of 1942 by Southern crews commencing to work the 10.55 am Exeter St David's-Taunton service, then taking over the 2.05 pm Taunton-Yeovil Pen Mill and returning with the 4.05 pm back before returning from Taunton to Exeter with the 6.25 pm. This duty was often being performed by a Southern 'T9' 4-4-0 locomotive. GWR 'Bulldog' 4-4-0s Nos. 3361, 3443 *Chaffinch*, and 3444 *Cormorant* of Taunton Shed also worked over the branch during the war years.

There was also a need for a direct connection between the Yeovil-Weymouth line and the Salisbury-Exeter line especially as plans for D-Day were being formulated - this was achieved on 13th October, 1943 with the opening of Yeovil South Junction (*see Chapter Eleven*).

Other engineering works had also taken place in the area in connection with the war effort. On 16th December, 1940 a fan of four sidings was open at Marston Magna to serve an ammunition depot situated on the down side, the existing goods siding being extended to form a reception siding and loop.

With food shortages and rationing there was a need for stores to hold emergency supplies. One of these depots, which were known as 'Buffer Stores', was established at Beer Hackett, on the up side 24 chains south of Thornford Bridge Halt and opened on 30th September, 1942 served by two sidings. Further War Department sidings were situated north of Sparkford station on the down side and were brought into use on 28th May, 1944.

During the war years the Signal & Telegraph department used a number of GWR camp coaches so that crews could be stationed at stratagic locations ready to undertake repairs at short notice. Between September and December 1942 no fewer than seven were recorded as being stationed at Yeovil Pen Mill, Nos. 9937, 9955, 9966, 9973, 9979, 9992, and 9998. Nos. 9955 and 9966 were reported as having moved to Westbury by February 1943, whilst Nos. 9977 and 9995 were at Marston Magna in November 1943.

Staff shortages caused by many railwaymen being in the services added to the daily toil of running a railway under war conditions. In 1943 it was recorded that the staff at Pen Mill consisted of 2 male and 2 female clerks, 36 male and 4 female wages grade staff. During that period many locomotives appeared which, under normal circumstances, did not operate in the Yeovil area. One example reported by the *Railway Observer* in the early summer of 1943 was the first recorded appearance of a Southern Railway 'Schools' class west of Salisbury, when No. 929 *Malvern* worked the 8.05 am stopping train from Salisbury to Exeter, returning with the 1.05 pm.

Severe weather caused an earth slip onto the down line ¾ mile south of Pen Mill on the morning of 31st January, 1943, single line working over the up line taking place between Pen Mill and Yetminster for several hours until the obstruction was cleared. A derailment at Yetminster on the 21st caused single working for a short while, and on 22nd February, 1944 an aircraft from Westland's airfield crashed on the Durston branch west of Hendford Halt, blocking the line for six hours.

Added to the many extra trains run for both the services and other Government departments, there were the specials for high ranking officers, General Eisenhower's private special train, code named 'Alive', passed over the Durston branch, arriving at Yeovil Town at 11.45 pm on 12th August, 1943. Here it was handed over to the Southern Railway to travel by an unspecified route to Bournemouth West and later Southampton Terminus. The train consisted of seven GWR bogies and two motorcar vans conveying six motorcars. General Montgomery's private special train, code named 'Rapier', was recorded as passing Yeovil Junction on at least three occasions. In the early hours of 19th November, 1943 it travelled from Addison Road, London, to Barnstaple Junction, returning that evening to Wilton, and again on 15th January, 1944 when it stopped overnight at Chard Junction before proceeding to Salisbury the following morning.

Other unusual workings often took place under the conditions created by the events of the time. Although they were not officially allowed over the Wilts, Somerset & Weymouth line south of Castle Cary owing to their route restriction status, more than one member of the GWR 2-8-0 '47XX' class worked through to Weymouth during that period!

During the early months of 1944 traffic increased even further in the build-up to D-Day, firstly with ammunition, equipment and stores being moved into temporary storage in the surrounding countryside prior to the final short journey to the channel ports and embarkation. Many hundreds of British and American soldiers were billeted at the Marston Magna site unloading train loads of ammunition which was stacked in the fields. But once the invasion was underway within 48 hours the massive stockpile had gone and the troops had departed, the camp and sidings having served their purpose.

In the run-up to the invasion troop trains appeared in great numbers, to be followed by a second movement as the invasion progressed, by which time traffic from the coast increased. A hospital train was based at Templecombe on the Southern line ready to move the many expected casualties, which fortunately were not as high as anticipated. Many were taken to the American Hospital erected at Coldharbour, Sherborne. Meanwhile, at Yeovil Pen Mill trainloads of German prisoners of war landed at Portland passed through *en route* to Devizes, these specials usually being hauled by one of Weymouth's '29XX' 'Saint' class locomotives.

In November 1944 Mr Leonard Hole, previously station master at Maiden Newton, moved to Yeovil Pen Mill to take control of that station.

During the autumn of 1945 the daily working by a Southern crew and locomotive over the Durston branch ceased. Following the years of war the naming of the 'West Country' class locomotive No. 21C104 (34004) *Yeovil* at Yeovil Town station on Friday 2nd November, 1945 was more than just a symbolic occasion. The nameplate was unveiled by the Mayor of Yeovil, Mr W.S. Vosper - himself an employee of the Southern Railway. Amongst officials of the company present were the Hon. Clive Pearson, a Director, and Mr O.V.S. Bulleid, the chief mechanical engineer who had designed the locomotive.

The previous month had seen the general re-introduction of restaurant cars on the Southern Railway, the GWR following on 31st December when passengers on selected services could again partake of full refreshments. The previous arrangements for working Southern Railway trains over the Yeovil-Durston branch were again put into operation on 8th September, 1946 following flooding of the main line, 'T9' class 4-4-0s and 2-6-0 moguls hauling the diverted trains which included the Plymouth-Portsmouth service and the 'Atlantic Coast Express'.

With the pressures of war removed attention again returned to locomotive performance. Having been absent from the Salisbury-Exeter line since pre-war days, on 17th September, 1946 'Lord Nelson' class No. 861 *Lord Anson* worked the 10.25 am Exeter-Waterloo service. The increased size and weight of engines was also giving problems for, until the strengthening of the bridge over the River Yeo near Yeovil Town during 1945, neither 'King Arthur' nor 'Merchant Navy' class locomotives could work into the station. During 1947 a 70 ft vacuum operated turntable replaced the original hand-propelled one at Yeovil Junction, to allow the turning of the Bulleid pacifics. At Pen Mill the first of the new GWR 4-6-0 'County' class to appear on the Wilts, Somerset & Weymouth line, No. 1025 *County of Radnor*, was recorded on a Weymouth-bound train early in the year.

Although the war was over, the country was for some years to be gripped by severe austerity as rationing and shortages continued. The blizzards that swept the Country on 19th January, 1947 and were to last with little respite for the next seven weeks added to the already existing difficulties as transport came to a halt and fuel supplies became unmovable. Although the Somerset/Dorset area was not as badly affected as other places, the GWR suspended certain main line and cross-country services from 27th January in order to provide extra locomotives for freight and to conserve coal. Those affected included the up and down Weymouth-Wolverhampton services, the 11.30 am Taunton-Yeovil and the 11.43 am Yeovil-Taunton.

Matters had eased a little by August when 300 children from two Sunday schools travelled to Weymouth for their annual outing - but at the same time 250 children from two other Sunday schools and an unrecorded number from another made the journey to Weymouth by motor coach! Despite petrol rationing the move away from the railways was again beginning to take place.

Although not referred to as the 'Atlantic Coast Express' in the timetable during the war years the basic train continued to run, indeed busier than in peacetime. It was not until October 1947 that the title reappeared in the timetable, the down train continuing to pass Yeovil Junction. The up train

The cramped conditions at Yeovil Town Shed are clearly demonstrated in this view, taken in the late 1940s, of 'T9' class 4-4-0 No. 307 standing ahead of the locomotive hoist. Two stacks and several wagonloads of coal are to be seen with the coal stage behind. *Author's Collection*

The Hon. Clive Pearson, Director of the Southern Railway Company, shakes hands with the Mayor of Yeovil, Mr W.S. Vosper, at the naming of 'West Country' class engine No. 21C104 (later 34004) *Yeovil* at Yeovil Town station on 2nd November, 1945. *Museum of South Somerset*

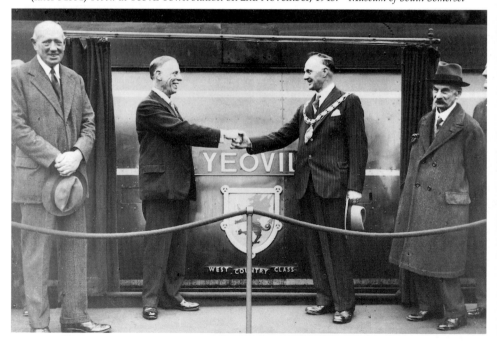

between Exeter and Salisbury stopped at Sidmouth Junction, Axminster, Yeovil Junction, Sherborne and Templecombe. At Yeovil Junction a coach brought from Yeovil Town by the branch shuttle was attached arriving at Waterloo at 4.41 pm.

Apart from the short experiment in the summer of 1880 the only Pullman regularly to run over the Salisbury-Exeter line was the 'Devon Belle'; this was an entirely different concept to the 'ACE'. First run on 20th June, 1947 it was an all-Pullman train complete with observation car, the only similarity to the 'ACE' was the fact it divided at Exeter Central, the front portion proceeding to Plymouth, the rear to Illfracombe.

One of the reasons for its introduction was the acute shortage of rolling stock which could be overcome with the Pullmans which had been stored throughout the war; seats could also be reserved which was not possible on ordinary trains at that time. Running only on Fridays, Saturdays, Sundays and Mondays with a supplementary fare of between 3s. 6d. and 8s., it appealed to those who could afford to pay and escape the dreariness of post-war rail travel. Although not stopping at Yeovil Junction it looked impressive as it sped through, usually headed by a 'Merchant Navy' class pacific.

The years immediately following the war were difficult for all as an austerity existence continued. The railways were in a thoroughly run-down state and in need of urgent investment after more than six years of intensive use with nothing but essential maintenance and were still under the control of the wartime Executive Committee. It was obvious that there would be no return to the old companies. The newly elected Labour Government was to nationalise the railways, coalmines, gas, and electricity undertakings, together with other industries.

Following the passing of the Transport Act on 6th August, 1947 the railways passed directly from the Executive Committee to the newly formed British Transport Commission on 1st January, 1948. The remit of the new Commission was wide ranging, for the setting up of a publicly owned system of on-land transport, including the take-over of railway and canal undertakings (including the London Passenger Transport Board) in a schedule which involved all main line railways and their joint committees, and smaller railway undertakings that were under the control of the Railway Executive Committee. Private owner wagons were transferred to the Commission with the exception of special types designed for specific traffics. The Commission also acquired road haulage undertakings engaged in predominantly long distance cartage for hire. Owing to the fact that the majority shares in the Tilling group of omnibus companies were owned by the former railway companies these also fell into the hands of the new Commission, which was empowered to make provision for area schemes for the co-ordination of passenger road transport. Politics and other changing factors were to intervene before the scheme was fully brought to fruition and it is a matter for conjecture how well it would have functioned had it proceeded.

Yeovil Pen Mill Shed taken from Wyndham Hill during August 1959, with the 44 ft turntable in the right foreground.   *Author*

Yeovil Pen Mill Shed during 1959, the sole occupant being a Western Region dmu. In the background a Bulleid light pacific can be seen, hauling a train from Yeovil Town to Yeovil Junction tender first.   *John Day*

Great Western Railway

As with the Bristol & Exeter, details of GWR broad gauge engines working in the Yeovil area are not fully recorded. Although the two-road engine shed of the GWR design of the period was erected for the opening of the line it seems that few engines were ever allocated there, and with the opening of the extension to Weymouth the shed was leased to the Bristol & Exeter who happened to own the land on which it stood! The sheds at Frome and Weymouth supplied the needs of the area.

Amongst the earliest engines working the Wilts, Somerset & Weymouth line were three members of the 2-2-2 'Fire Fly' class, *Mentor, Arrow* and *Lethe*, built in 1841/2. They were reported as being unsuitable for the climb to Evershot and other gradients on the line. The 'Leo' class 2-4-0 goods engines also appeared in the early days, and the 'Waverley' class, built in 1855, made occasional appearances, these being the only 4-4-0 tender engines to run on the broad gauge.

New engines to work the line included the 2-4-0 'Victoria' class, until they were superseded by the Armstrong 2-4-0 'Hawthorn' class whose active life continued until the end of the broad gauge in 1892. It was the removal of the broad gauge from the Wilts, Somerset & Weymouth section in 1874, and the absorption by the GWR of the Bristol & Exeter company in 1876, that brought the Yeovil shed (and land) into GWR ownership by which time the standard gauge engines of the GWR were allocated. These were a few of the smaller tender types but mostly they were assorted saddle- and side-tank varieties.

Of the more unusual allocations to Pen Mill were several former Monmouthshire Railway & Canal Company locomotives. Taken over by the GWR in 1880 and rebuilt later by that company, they made infrequent appearances in the Weymouth and Yeovil area. During 1902 Nos. 1308, 1309, and 1310 were all (at various times during the year) allocated to Weymouth, Bridport and Yeovil.

By 1906 the allocation consisted of 12 locomotives: three tender engines Armstrong 2-4-0 Nos. 2207, 2208 and Dean Goods 0-6-0 No. 2315; two 'Metro' 2-4-0 tanks, Nos. 1453 and 1495; three 'Buffalo' '1076' class 0-6-0 saddle tanks, Nos. 1178, 1587, 1606; and four '2721' class 0-6-0 saddle tanks, Nos. 2745, 2767, 2770, and 2795.

The requirements had not changed in 1921 when 11 engines were in residence: three tender engines, '3521' class 4-4-0 No. 3552 and two 'Dean Goods' 0-6-0 Nos. 2339 and 2410, three 'Metro' 2-4-0 tanks Nos. 459, 624 and 626 all of the earlier variety with inside bearings to their leading wheels; No. 3576 an 0-4-2 tank of the '3571' class, two 'Buffalo' '1076' class tanks Nos. 1250 and 1626 and '1854/1701' class 0-6-0 saddle tank No. 1761. Looking the most modern was '1813' class pannier tank No. 1835 having been converted from a saddle tank the previous year, and going on to record the highest mileage of its class, 1,068,029 when withdrawn in 1949.

Unable to turn tender engines with a total wheelbase of over 44 ft, Pen Mill shed was at a disadvantage. During 1928 extension bars (known as 'skids') were fitted and engines up to the size of a mogul could be accommodated with the rear end of the tender propelled up the skids, the unbalanced table then being turned only with great difficulty!

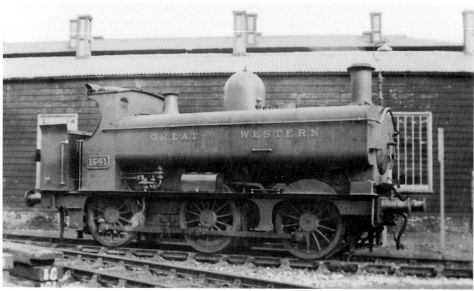

'1501' class 0-6-0 tank No. 1541 stands on the turntable road of Yeovil Pen Mill Shed. Originally constructed as a saddle tank in February 1880 and converted to a pannier tank in April 1920, she retained her open cab until withdrawn in December 1937.   *Author's Collection*

'45XX' class 2-6-2 tank No. 4507 stands inside Yeovil Pen Mill shed on 22nd May, 1955.
R.K. Blencowe

Moving forward to March 1933 there was not a saddle tank to be seen, all having been rebuilt as pannier tanks. Four 'Buffalo' '1076' class Nos. 1239, 1565, 1598 and 1620 formed the mainstay of the nine engines allocated, plus one '645/1501' class tank No. 1538 and '813' class No. 1816, 2-4-0 'Metro' tank No. 986 and double-framed '2361' class 0-6-0 tender engine No. 2364 was seeing out her final year in service, whilst '45XX' 2-6-2 tank No. 4551 had arrived.

Nine months later an ever-changing allocation left only two 'Buffalo' tanks from the previous year - Nos. 1598 and 1620. However, they had been joined by Nos. 1166, 1179, 1180, and 1624, giving the shed six of these engines which were known for their free running qualities. Two other pannier tanks - '645/1501' class No. 1525 and '1854' class No. 1860 - remained and were joined by '45XX' class tanks Nos. 5548 and 5554.

The following year the position had again changed, only three of the previous 'Buffalo' tanks remained, Nos. 1179, 1598, and 1624, but were joined by four '1701/1854' Dean single frame pannier tanks - Nos. 907, 1706, 1710 and 1881 - and 'Dean Goods' No. 2518, an engine which had been sent to France during World War I and was destined to return there in 1940 as WD 104. The two '4575' class 2-6-2 tanks were joined by '45XX' class No. 4566, today still running in preservation on the Severn Valley Railway.

The old order was changing and by January 1938 two '57XX' class pannier tanks Nos. 8714 and 9759 had arrived to join 2-6-2 tanks Nos. 4536, 5509 and 5565. The next youngest engine, '2721' class pannier tank No. 2779, dated from 1900 whilst the oldest from 1880 was the remaining 'Buffalo' tank No. 1615, and one '655' class No. 2703 worked with three '1854' class pannier tanks, Nos. 907, 1729 and 1758. The sole remaining tender engine, 'Dean Goods' No. 2456, was sent to France in 1940 as WD 114, and as with No. 2518, upon return in 1945 both were broken up.

Throughout the war years there were many engine changes. Yeovil pannier tank No. 1729 was bombed at Castle Cary in 1942 to become one of only two GWR locomotives completely destroyed as a result of enemy action. Nine engines were allocated during 1944 with only two of the rebuilt former saddle tanks remaining - Nos. 1767 and 1895 of the '1854' class. The other five pannier tanks were of modern construction, Nos. 3671, 3733, 5767, 8745, and 9771, the allocation being completed by two '4575' class 2-6-2 tanks Nos. 5529 and 5565.

The last two Victorian engines departed in 1947 with the withdrawal of Nos. 1767 and 1895, and on the eve of Nationalisation the final GWR allocation consisted of seven '57XX' class pannier tanks, Nos. 3671, 3733, 4689, 5767, 9601, 9615, 9771, one '45XX' 2-6-2 tank No. 4572, and two '4575' class Nos. 5529 and 5565.

The operating requirement had dropped to nine engines by July 1953 - six pannier tanks, Nos. 3671, 3733, 4689, 8745, 9601 and 9732, with three '4575' class 2-6-2 tanks, Nos. 5529, 5565, 5567 - a requirement that was to remain until the shed's closure in January 1959.

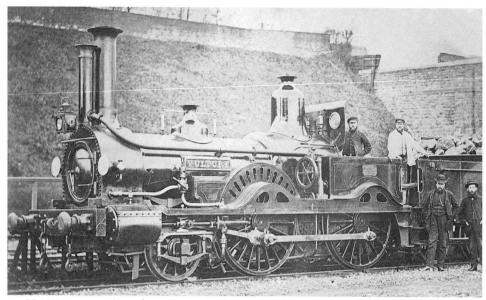

No. 69 *Argus* one of Joseph Beattie's 'Falcon' class of 2-4-0 passenger engines fitted with 6 ft 6 in. driving wheels. *Argus*, built in April 1863, survived until May 1886, and when withdrawn had travelled a recorded 704,961 miles. Photographed at Exeter Queen Street, this petite engine, with its lack of protection for the crew, would have hauled the Salisbury-Exeter trains of the period.

Author's Collection

Photographed at Exeter, complete with 'pup' chimney and feed water heater, No. 30 *Vulture* was one of three engines of the 2-4-0 'Eagle' class. Built in 1862 at a cost of £2,965 each, with their 6 ft driving wheels they worked Exeter-Salisbury expresses until 1870. Reduced to secondary duties, *Vulture*, after travelling a recorded 599,967 miles, was withdrawn in December 1886.

Author's Collection

LSWR and Southern Railway

The opening of the line to Yeovil and the extension to Exeter required extra engines at Salisbury and an allocation to Yeovil and Exeter. For the opening various 2-2-2 singles of the 'Mazeppa' class were sent to Yeovil, Nos. 53 *Mazeppa*, 58 *Sultan*, and 61 *Snake*. They were then 13 years old and past their prime. Other singles included three members of the 2-2-2 'Canute' class, Nos. 149 *Napoleon*, 151 *Montrose*, and 152 *Marmion*. The latter became derailed near Gillingham on 20th November, 1860. Disaster also befell Yeovil-based 'Bison' class 0-6-0 No. 103 *Tiger*, which likewise left the rails near Honiton on 29th July, 1860, both derailments being blamed on excessive speed on a newly opened line.

Another 2-2-2 single allocated to Yeovil was No. 114 *Frome* - one of the Christie, Adams, & Hill locomotives. *Frome* was famed for three events: heading the opening train between Gillingham and Sherborne on 7th May, 1860, the following year hauling the special conveying the Prince of Wales (later King Edward V11) from Havant to Gosport following the death of Prince Albert, and thirdly the well-documented photograph taken of the engine in Yeovil yard on 8th August, 1862, the results of which brought driver Hicks a severe reprimand for the unauthorised use of the engine to obtain the photograph and consumption of coke, oil and water.

Slightly larger 2-4-0s with 6 ft 6 in. driving wheels were also allocated to Yeovil. No. 173 *Nymph* of the 'Undine' class arrived in 1863 and the following year No. 69 *Argus* of the 'Falcon' class - although the latter engine is also credited with being based at Exeter! However, along with other members of the class, she certainly worked over the Salisbury-Exeter line at that period.

No. 235 of the '231' class of 2-4-0s went to Yeovil new in August 1866 and the following year was regularly working the Yeovil-Waterloo milk vans and Exeter van trains. By 1872 2-4-0s Nos. 25 *Reindeer* and 91 *Spitfire* of the 'Volcano' class were recorded as working considerable distances including a Yeovil-Torrington working; *Reindeer* regularly handled the 6.15 am Yeovil-Waterloo semi-fast, returning at 2.10 pm with an express as far as Salisbury. No. 84 *Styx* of the 'Falcon' class was also at that time working principal trains from Yeovil, and despite the appearance of newer engines, 'Undine' class No. 168 *Electra* was at Yeovil in 1878, whilst several members of the 2-4-0 'Tweed' class ended their days there in the late 1870s. 'Saxon' class 4-4-0 No. 137 *Hun* spent her final days at Yeovil until withdrawn in December 1885, having achieved a total mileage of 723,027.

Goods locomotives also featured in Yeovil's allocation from the earliest days. In 1863 two members of the 'Gem' class of 2-4-0 goods engines, Nos. 55 *Medusa* and 57 *Meteor*, went new to Yeovil. In August 1872 'Lion' class 0-6-0 No. 16 *Salisbury* was sent new to Yeovil where (unusually for an 0-6-0) she often worked semi-fast passenger trains to and from Exeter. The old chestnut concerning little old ladies wishing to go to Salisbury boarding any train that No. 16 happened to be hauling caused her name to be changed to *Stonehenge* in August 1877.

March 1878 saw four members of the Beyer, Peacock double-framed 0-6-0 goods engines allocated to Yeovil, Nos. 221 *Scotia*, 225 *Hibernia*, 242 and 286. These were well constructed engines which served the company well, and they were much modified over the years. Single-framed Beyer, Peacock 0-6-0 goods engines Nos. 339 and 340 were also allocated new to Yeovil in the same year. Two

Christie Adams & Hill 6 ft 6 in. single No. 114 *Frome* photographed at Yeovil Town on 8th August, 1862. On the footplate is driver Hicks who commissioned a local photographer to take the picture. Upon hearing of the exploit London & South Western management were displeased at the unauthorised use of the engine consuming coke, oil and water. Hicks received a severe reprimand after handing over the photographs. However, the management were not quick witted enough to demand the negative, hence Hicks and railway historians had the last laugh!

Museum of South Somerset

'A12' class 'Jubilee' 0-4-2T No. 554 stands outside Yeovil Town Shed. Built in December 1889 at a cost of £2,225, the engine is shown here in Adams pre-1893 livery displaying 5¼ inch lettering 'L&SWR' on the tender and fitted with the original stove pipe chimney. In the background rises Summerhouse Hill, whilst in the foreground is track laid on longitudinal sleepers with a revolving disc shunting signal near the cab. These date this view as nineteenth century.

Leslie Brooke Collection

members of the 2-4-0 'Vesuvius' class, No. 19 *Briton* and 20 *Princess*, had been allocated to Yeovil by June 1883 to work secondary passenger and local duties.

After 1878 the new engines of Adams graced the lines of the South Western, Yeovil usually receiving an allocation once the passenger classes were past their first prime. One of the few exceptions to the rule was class '460' 4-4-0 No. 476 which arrived new in August 1884. Conversely, older engines seeing out their final years included 'Undine' class 2-4-0s Nos. 172 *Zephyr* and 175 *Hebe*, both withdrawn from Yeovil in late 1886.

The introduction of the 'Jubilee' 'A12' class 0-4-2 tender engines in 1887 saw trials carried out on the Salisbury-Yeovil line with prototype No. 527, including working a Yeovil-London milk train. Yeovil was allocated two of the class new in 1889 - Nos. 551 and 553 - and between them they worked a daily van train to Clapham Junction, returning with a goods via Eastleigh, a duty they maintained for over 10 years. In October and November 1893 Nos. 537 and 615 took part in coal consumption trials, working the Nine Elms-Yeovil fast goods. October 1891 saw double-framed Beyer, Peacock goods No. 242 condemned from Yeovil Shed having covered only 603,165 miles, the lowest recorded for the class.

'T3' class 4-4-0 No. 571, new in August 1893, arrived at Yeovil early the following year, principally to work the Waterloo milk trains on which the loads were becoming too heavy for the 'Jubilees'. She was joined by No. 575 the following year. Single-framed Beyer, Peacock 0-6-0 goods No. 343 had arrived by March 1895, and a year later Nos. 471 and 474 of the '460' class 4-4-0s with 6 ft 7 in. driving wheels were at Yeovil.

Members of the '380' class 4-4-0s with 5 ft 7 in. driving wheels, a class reputed to give a mediocre performance and known by the crews as 'Steamrollers,' had arrived by the late 1890s with the allocation of Nos. 287, 288 and 389. Renumbered with the prefix 0 during 1902, No. 0386 joined the other three at that time.

The first recorded allocation of 'G6' 0-6-0 tanks to Yeovil was in March 1901 with Nos. 240 and 266, one usually being sub-shedded at Templecombe for shunting duties - a practice that was to continue for the next 49 years.

In June 1902 Yeovil had two of the Drummond 'T9' 4-4-0 express engines, Nos. 286 and 703. It was an association with the depot that was to last for over 50 years. They were known as the 'Greyhounds' for their free running qualities and speed, which gained them a reputation over the undulating Salisbury-Exeter route. Members of the 'K10' 4-4-0 mixed traffic class, with their smaller driving wheels of 5 ft 7 in., were known to the crews as the 'Small Hoppers'. No. 381 had arrived by 1904, with various members being at Yeovil throughout the life of the class. By mid-1910 Nos. 664 and 666, two members of the Adams 'X6' class 4-4-0s with 6 ft 7 in. driving wheels, had been allocated to Yeovil for working the 8.41 am Yeovil Junction-Waterloo slow, returning with the 2.25 pm Wimbledon-Templecombe milk vans. Rebuilt single-framed Beyer, Peacock goods No. 0229 had also been allocated, to be joined the following year by '460' class No. 478, and the 1912 allocation of 'T9s' consisted of Nos. 116, 117, and 300.

Events during World War I caused alterations to many existing arrangements, many unfortunately not recorded. However, in August 1918 two members of the 'X2' class of 4-4-0 express engines, Nos. 577 and 585, were noted as working milk trains from Yeovil. A class built in 1890 with 7 ft 1 in. driving

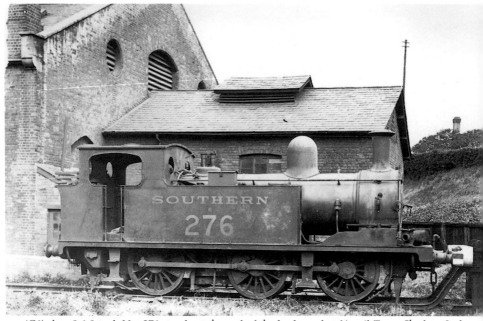

'G6' class 0-6-0 tank No. 276 stands at the end of the back road at Yeovil Town Shed on 2nd August, 1928. Built in August 1900 and after a working life of 49 years, No. 276 was withdrawn in October 1949. Behind can be seen the short two-road extension to the back of the shed.

H.C. Casserley

'K10' class 4-4-0 No. 380 (*left*) and 'L11' class 4-4-0 No. 439 (*right*) stand in the back of Yeovil Town Shed on 12th June, 1926. The archways cut into the rear wall leading to the short extension shown above are clearly visible. *H.C. Casserley*

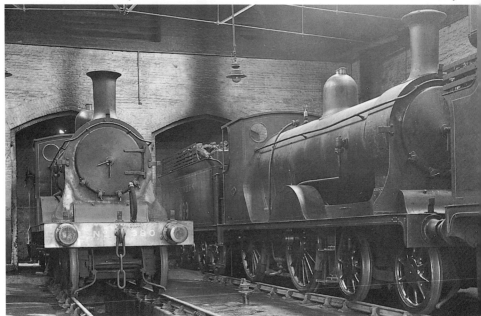

seven 'U' class moguls, four pannier tanks, two '4575' 2-6-2 tanks and two 'M7s'. Five of the moguls - Nos. 31610, 31623, 31626, 31790, and 31791 - departed the following month but were replaced by others of the class and the allocation was constantly changing. By November 1960 the number of allocated engines had dropped to 14, including No. 4507 - the oldest GWR engine in regular service!

The change of control to the Western Region in 1963 was to see the demise of the final LSWR engines with the departure of 'M7' tanks Nos. 30052 and 30129, after which the 'U' class were the sole representives of the former Southern Railway. In the October of the same year No. 4507 departed for the scrap yard, the last engine built at Wolverhampton Stafford Road works to be in service, having been completed in May 1907. During the early 1950s she had been allocated for short periods to both Taunton and Yeovil before moving to Weymouth where she was usually sub-shedded at Bridport until 1959, moving to Yeovil the following year. When withdrawn it was estimated she had travelled 1,189,165 miles. The Wolverhampton press suggested that a fund be started to purchase her for preservation, but unfortunately this idea was not taken up, and on 15th July, 1964 she entered the yard of Bird Bros, Pontymister. By the end of the month a unique engine had gone.

The overall reduction of services and closures involved a constant changing of allocation as engines were withdrawn and others moved to fill their places. The remaining 'U' class were withdrawn in 1963/4 to be replaced by Standard class '4' 4-6-0s, and by mid-1964 three former LMS class '3' 2-6-2 tanks - Nos. 41283, 41290, and 41295 - had arrived at Yeovil. In late 1961 a batch of Standard class '4' 2-6-4 tanks had also arrived at Taunton and commenced duties on the Durston-Yeovil branch, several members of the class also being allocated to Yeovil for short periods, including Nos. 80035, 80038 and 80039, the former being withdrawn from Yeovil Shed in April 1965.

In early 1964 several members of the class '22' 'D63XX' diesel-hydraulics were based at Taunton, often putting in appearances on Yeovil branch trains, and other duties whilst at Yeovil, including banking to Evershot, but they were never allocated to Yeovil, which was soon to become little more than a sub-shed of both Salisbury and Exmouth Junction. The reduced allocation reflected in engines from both of these depots working at Yeovil.

Yeovil Town Shed closed to steam on 12th June, 1965 after which it remained as a stabling point. Apart from the Yeovil Junction shuttle railcar and a diesel shunter, the reduction of services was soon to reduce drastically the requirements for other engines. Thus 104 years of history ended; Yeovil's own allocation had covered the history of the LSWR, always a Mecca for visiting engines lying over between duties and - following post-war bridge strengthening - 'S15' 4-6-0 mixed traffic engines along with the 'King Arthur' class and Bulleid's light pacifics were to be regular visitors. By the nature of its location it was always a stopping off point for West Country engines *en route* to and from Eastleigh works, especially the smaller tank engines such as the 'B4' 0-4-0s and the three Wadebridge-based Beattie well tanks.

Other unusual visitors to be seen at times included a Stanier '8F' 2-8-0, a GWR 'Castle' class that had failed on the Weymouth line, '9F' class 2-10-0 *Evening Star*, and various main line diesels also often appeared in later days. Now gone

BR Standard '3MT' 2-6-2 tank No. 82042 approaches Yeovil Town station with the 12.58 pm Taunton-Yeovil Pen Mill train on 17th February, 1962. To the left is the original LSWR line to Hendford reduced to a siding and to the right the premises of Messrs Blake & Fox, glove manufacturers.   *John Day*

The final line up and representative of the British Railways Standard classes that were allocated to Yeovil in later years. Standard class '4' 4-6-0 No. 75005 hauls a line of dead engines consisting of Nos. 41290, 75003, 82035, 80035, 9670 and 73166 on 13th June, 1965. The previous day Yeovil Town Shed had closed as a steam depot, thus ending another chapter in the station's history.
                                                                                                    John Day

forever, the panoramic view of the shed obtained from Summerhouse Hill will be an abiding memory for many Yeovil people.

During the early years Yeovil was also host to locomotives of the Engineer's Department used in the maintenance of the line, but whether these engines shared accommodation at Yeovil Town Shed or were isolated in some other structure is open to conjecture.

The first three such engines to appear were *Hesketh*, *Locke* and *Smeaton* - all 2-4-0 long boilered 0-6-0 tender engines built by George England. *Hesketh* came in 1859, and the other two in 1861 during which year it was recorded that *Locke* was employed on the Colyton (Seaton Junction) slip, *Smeaton* on the Yeovil-Exeter doubling and *Hesketh* on Yeovil-Exeter maintenance work. In December 1870 *Hesketh* was allocated to Yeovil and *Locke* and *Smeaton* to Exeter.

Yolland, an 0-6-0 goods engine built by Stephenson in 1866 and transferred to the Engineer's Department in 1875, was reported as working on relaying work between Milborne Port and Yeovil Junction during 1877, whilst *Hesketh* was laid up following a derailment at Yeovil Junction. She was broken up the following year and replaced by a former Somerset & Dorset George England 2-4-0, No. 14A, which received the name *Fowler*. The use of separate Engineer's engines ceased after 1888, when it was decided that all motive power be the responsibility of one department.

No further involvement with engineer's locomotives occurred until 1965 when a permanent way yard was established on ground to the north side of Yeovil Junction. To shunt this facility DS 1169 - a 4-wheel Ruston-Hornsby diesel-mechanical shunter (No. 237923) of 1946 - arrived. Originally at Folkestone Warren until 1959, she then moved to Broad Clyst sleeper depot until its closure in 1964. From there she went to Taunton before arriving in Yeovil the following year, remaining there until withdrawn in March 1972, and passing to Cohen of Cransley, Northants, in June 1973.

Permanent way department diesel shunter No. DS1169, a 48 hp Ruston-Hornsby of 1946 vintage, is seen shunting a wagon load of sleepers in the permanent way yard at Yeovil Junction on 5th March, 1969. *Author*

Chapter Eleven

Signalling

Bristol & Exeter Railway and Great Western Railway

Generally, the signalling arrangements of the Bristol & Exeter Railway followed GWR practice, as the latter company had worked the line initially. Double disc-and-crossbars were used at junctions together with a modified type of disc signal where the disc was swung to a horizontal position, which was introduced as an auxiliary or distant signal. Although the company's signal engineer was Gregory, who had been the instigator of the semaphore as a railway signal, none was installed on the Bristol & Exeter lines until after the GWR had taken over.

The Electric Telegraph had been installed on the Durston-Yeovil branch from its opening, and after 1865 Absolute Block working was introduced using Tyer's instruments. Starting signals were then installed on both the main line and branches, but interlocking of points and signals was slow to develop within the company - although by the mid-1870s many 'Block Huts' (the name signal boxes were officially called on the Bristol & Exeter) had been erected, usually equipped with Saxby & Farmer locking frames.

The first signal boxes appeared on the Durston-Yeovil branch during 1874 when they were erected at Durston and Langport. A box appeared at Martock around 1880 and in 1881 others were constructed at Athelney and Hendford. Montacute box opened in January 1882.

It would appear that interlocking had been progressively introduced down the branch from Durston, a Signalling Committee meeting in December 1880 being told that it was desirable to introduce locking at Yeovil Town. On 23rd February, 1881 both the GWR and LSWR agreed that the antiquated signalling at Yeovil Town, which consisted of two boxes at either end of the layout (one for each company), should be replaced by modern equipment at an estimated cost of £1,536 to be shared by both companies.

On 30th March, 1882 the two new boxes came into operation, thus removing the final disc-and-crossbar signals from both Hendford and Yeovil Town. At the latter one had served as the up distant signal and was almost at Pen Mill, whilst others had controlled LSWR trains. Yeovil Town East box, with a 24-lever frame situated on the Yeovil Pen Mill side of Newton Road bridge in the vee where the Pen Mill and Yeovil Junction lines divided, controlled the Durston branch from Yeovil Town West to Yeovil Pen Mill South and LSWR trains to and from Yeovil Junction and the shunting movements at the east end of the station. Yeovil Town West with a 37-lever frame was situated to the north side of the Durston branch between the points leading to the goods yard and the footbridge from Stars Lane to Summerhouse Hill. The box controlled the single line to Hendford, all shunting movements at the west end of the station, the goods yard and engine shed. Owing to the short distance between the two boxes (approximately 250 yds) many of the signals were slotted by both boxes (both signalmen had to co-operate to operate return it to the original point of issue. Although several trains could be sent in the same direction in succession with a ticket - the last carrying the staff - it was not the ideal solution. The Board of Trade failed to force its introduction, but the company did begrudgingly later begin to introduce it and by May 1877 the Weymouth line was so equipped and with signals and signal boxes, all points and signals being interlocked and worked from within the boxes.

Two boxes were erected at Yeovil Pen Mill - 'No. 1' at the north end of the station, on the north side of the main line near the goods shed, and 'No. 2' situated in the vee of the junction of the Weymouth line and the Yeovil Town branch. No. 1 box, later renamed 'North Box' had a 24-lever frame of which 17 were in use, and No. 2 box (becoming 'South Box') had a 21-lever frame, 18 of which were in use. Signal boxes either side of Pen Mill were Marston Magna to the north and Yetminster to the south. All of these boxes were built with brick bases and wooden tops and are classed as 'GWR type 2' by the Signalling Record Society.

The exact details of the original arrangements for the junction of the Clifton Maybank spur are not available. A box had been provided by 1877 although it was not classed as a block post and was manned only as required. A note in the working timetable stated that Clifton Maybank could only be used during the hours of daylight, which suggests that the signals were not equipped with lamps. The original signal box was replaced in 1896 by a new structure containing a double twist locking frame with 21 levers spaced at 5¼ inch centres. The layout was simplified in January 1931 when the loop at the commencement of the branch was taken out of use. Following the closure of the branch, the box closed on 1st November, 1937 and was removed the following month.

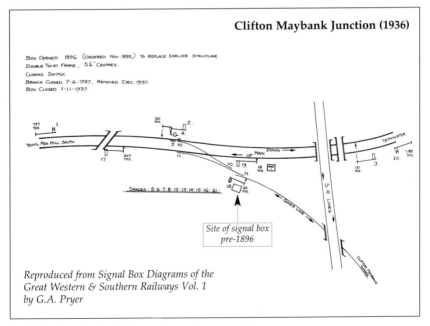

Clifton Maybank Junction (1936)

Box Opened 1896 (Ordered Nov. 1895) to Replace Earlier Structure.
Double Twist Frame, 5¼" Centres.
Closing Switch.
Branch Closed 7-6-1937, Removed Dec. 1937.
Box Closed 1-11-1937.

Spaces: 5:6:7:8:12:13:14:15:16:21:

Site of signal box
pre-1896

Reproduced from Signal Box Diagrams of the Great Western & Southern Railways Vol. 1 by G.A. Pryer

The situation at Yeovil Town changed little since the alterations of 1882, but at a meeting of the Joint Committee in November 1915 it was decided that, owing to unsatisfactory view of the lines and signals from the West signal box and in order to effect economy, a new joint box should be provided at an estimated cost of £1,400 replacing both East and West boxes. This would save the wages of three signalmen estimated at £264 per annum. The new box came into use on 20th October, 1916 and was of standard GWR design of brick construction with a hip roof, classified by the Signalling Record Society as a GWR type 7D. The box was equipped with a vertical tappet 3-bar lever frame containing 55 levers at 4 inch centres. The single line sections to Hendford and Yeovil Pen Mill were controlled by Webb-Thompson electric train staff, although later the section to Pen Mill was converted to electric key token. The double line section to Yeovil Junction 'A' (and later Yeovil South Junction) was operated with Preece's one-wire Block, later updated to three-wire. Few alterations took place to the signalling until the Southern Region took full control during 1950, after which signal replacements were of the Southern type and the signal box acquired a Southern Region green enamel nameplate 'Yeovil Town' replacing the previous GWR cast type which left nobody in any doubt that they were looking at 'Yeovil Town Signal Box'. No further alterations took place until after the closure of the Durston branch, when on 12th September, 1965 part of the single line to Hendford was removed and the goods line connected to Hendford Siding (the former LSWR line to Hendford) by hand points. Following the withdrawal of the Yeovil Town-Yeovil Junction shuttle in October 1966 and the subsequent lifting of the track towards Yeovil Junction Yeovil Town signal box closed on 1st March, 1967, the line from Yeovil Pen Mill being operated as a siding.

The arrangements at Pen Mill had remained intact until late 1936 when construction work commenced on a new box at the Marson Magna end of the island platform. It was of brick construction and is classified as GWR type 11 by the Signalling Record Society, containing a vertical tappet (VT) 5-bar frame of 65 levers at 4 inch centres. The change-over from the previous North and South boxes was spread over seven days, North box closing on 14th February, 1937 whilst South box - although disconnected on the 17th - remained a block post until the 21st. Signalling over the main line was maintained with GWR Spangnoletti block instruments, and the single line section to Yeovil Town employed the electric key token (colour green). As with the previous boxes, both the up and down distant signals were fixed at caution owing to the speed restrictions through the station.

The next development came as a result of the war when Yeovil South Junction opened on 13th October, 1943. Situated 1,000 yards south of Yeovil Pen Mill this box of standard GWR ARP design (designated 'GWR type 13' by the Signalling Record Society) controlled a double track connection from the Yeovil Pen Mill-Weymouth line to the Yeovil Town-Yeovil Junction line from a northerly direction. It was equipped with a 33-lever VT 5-bar locking frame at 4 inch centres which allowed for a second connection giving through running from the Weymouth direction to Yeovil Town, but this was never installed. The complete installation, which cost £9,045, was open only for special traffic, diversions and broke her crank axle at Crewkerne whilst working the 4.30 pm Exeter-Waterloo express. The entire class was withdrawn for inspection, LNER 'V2' class 2-6-2s and British Railways 'Britannia' class 4-6-2s taking over many workings on the Waterloo-Exeter line.

It was not until October 1951 that a new era dawned (briefly) on the Salisbury-Exeter line with the introduction of main line diesel-electric locomotives on certain services. Following trials, Southern Region 1-Co-Co-1 No. 10202 made its first service run on 17th October with the down 'ACE', returning with the 4.30 pm from Exeter. Later she was joined by No. 10201 which had been exhibited at the Festival of Britain and they commenced duties which also involved workings on Waterloo-Bournemouth-Weymouth services.

In March and April 1953 the two former LMS Co-Co diesel electric locomotives Nos. 10000 and 10001 were transferred to the Southern Region, taking over the workings of the Southern locomotives. As with their predecessors, they put up some spectacular performances although there were various problems with these advanced machines and appearances were at times intermittent! On 12th September No. 10000, working the 2.30 pm from Exeter, failed at Yeovil Junction, the train proceeding with a steam locomotive hastily summoned from Yeovil Town.

The third Southern locomotive, No. 10203, hauled 12-coach test trains between Waterloo and Exeter on 6th and 7th May, 1954, taking the 9 am Waterloo-Exeter as its first passenger service on the 10th.

By January 1955 only No. 10001 was on the Exeter route working the 1.33 am and 1 pm down services, and the 7.30 am and 5.33 pm return services from Exeter to Waterloo. By the end of March both locomotives had returned to the Midland Region, no further diesels appearing until the declining days of steam. Novel at the time, they had provided much useful information for the future modernisation programme and richly deserve their place in railway history.

Reverting back to 1950 the first operational changes were taking place. From 2nd April the first change of Regional boundaries took place, the former Wilts, Somerset & Weymouth line from just south of Castle Cary to Weymouth including branch lines was transferred to the Southern Region. This included the Durston branch to a point west of Langport West, although for operational reasons the motive power depots at Yeovil Pen Mill and Weymouth remained under the control of the Western Region, having received the British Railways shed codes of 82E and 82F respectively. Again to the public there was little outward change, but the words 'Southern Region' appeared on paperwork, stations and other buildings received green and cream paintwork upon repainting, and on the signalling side replacement signals were of the SR upper quadrant pattern, often mounted on SR rail-built signal posts.

Despite these changes traffic continued much as before, 25th September saw the re-introduction of slip coaches for Weymouth off the 10.30 am and 3.30 pm West of England expresses from Paddington. Early 1951 saw the re-introduction to the Weymouth line of the former GWR twin-car diesel railcar set Nos. 35 & 36. With a composite coach marshalled between them, this three-coach train worked the 8.05 am Bristol Temple Meads-Weymouth service, returning at 12.35 pm. It was, however, short lived and intermittent, the unit often being out of service through mechanical problems.

Although photographed in the early 1950s this scene has a real LSWR/SR flavour. No. 30449 *Sir Torre* awaits departure from Yeovil Junction with a down train consisting of Maunsell stock, the engine retaining an LSWR 'watercart' 8-wheel tender. No. 30449 was originally built in December 1910 as a 'P14' class 4-6-0, withdrawn in October 1927 after 433,147 miles and rebuilt at a cost of £6,320 as an 'N15' 4-6-0 of the 'King Arthur' class. Very little of the original engine remained. Even then bookkeeping exercises were performed! Re-entering service in June 1925 as No. 449 and named *Sir Torre* she represented the Southern Railway at the Stockton & Darlington Centenary celebrations, being finally withdrawn in December 1959 having travelled 1,373,426 recorded miles. Note the rather splendid starting signal with co-acting arms for the through line!

G.M. Stubbs

One of Bulleid's controversial 'Battle of Britain' class 4-6-2 No. 34056 *Croydon* stands at Yeovil Junction with an up stopping train consisting of four Maunsell coaches in British Railways 'blood & custard' livery. Behind the station name board stand Bulleid coaches in British Railways' version of Southern Green. *Croydon* was built in February 1947 as No. 21C156, renumbered in May 1948 and rebuilt in December 1960. Finally withdrawn from service in May 1967, she had run a recorded 957,081 miles in 20 years.

G.M. Stubbs

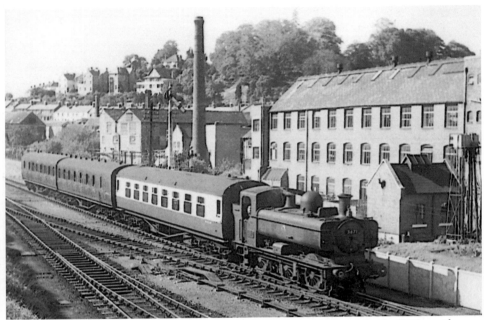

Ex-GWR '57XX' class 0-6-0 pannier tank No. 3671 approaches Dodham Lane footbridge with a train off the Durston branch.   *G.M. Stubbs*

Winter morning at Hendford Halt, with frost on the wooden platform and sleepers and the faint winter sun throwing shadows as '45XX' class 2-6-2 tank No. 4507 arrives with a train from Taunton on 11th December, 1954. Behind are the lorries of a haulage contractor in the former yard of the Ham Hill & Doulting Stone Company. In the background is the Westland factory, today Yeovil's principal employer.   *G.M. Stubbs*

Yeovil Pen Mill, looking north on 2nd March, 1956. The tight clearance of the up line between the two platforms is evident. On the left a '4575' class 2-6-2 tank waits to depart with a Taunton train. Situated on the platform alongside the telegraph pole is the cabinet containing the auxiliary key token machine for the Yeovil Pen Mill-Yeovil Town section; with its door open the machine is just visible. *H.C. Casserley*

A general view of Yeovil Pen Mill on 7th July, 1957, looking south, with the Sherborne Road bridge forming the end of the picture. A train is just departing in the Weymouth direction. The running-in board on the island platform clearly proclaims 'change for Taunton & Exeter'. *H.C. Casserley*

On 8th October, 1955 '43XX' class 2-6-0 No. 6351 with a Weymouth-bound goods stands at Yeovil Pen Mill down starting signal whilst GWR railcar No. W28 departs from the up platform for Weymouth. The route indicator on the signal on the left would be showing 'DM'. After passing under the bridge the train will gain the down line via the crossover.   *G.M. Stubbs*

As with the above photograph, on 27th May, 1961 '57XX' 0-6-0 tank No. 8745 with a Taunton-bound train has departed Yeovil Pen Mill from the up line. The layout required these movements to take the down line for a few feet before gaining the branch, thus blocking the entire south end of the station. A facility to run straight back onto the Yeovil Town line would have greatly eased the signalman's problems!   *Author*

Weymouth-based '14XX' class 0-4-2 tank No. 1467 after working a trip between Pen Mill and Yeovil Town shunts clear of the Durston platform on 10th July, 1956. In the background a 'U' class mogul shunts the goods yard. The sight of a GWR locomotive and auto-coach, GWR signal box and signals belies the fact that Yeovil Town was essentially a Southern Railway establishment.   *R.C. Riley*

A '4575' class 2-6-2 tank heads through the cutting towards Hendford with an evening train from Yeovil Pen Mill to Taunton in October 1959. The coaches are just passing under Nursery bridge, beyond which is the stone bridge carrying Hendford Hill over the railway. The former LSWR line (reduced to a siding) is on the right.   *Author*

Yeovil Town Council at their meeting on Monday 13th April unanimously agreed to request that the line should remain open until the end of October, one member feeling that this would particularly benefit those planning to travel to Minehead and Weston-super-Mare, whilst several criticized the additional bus services. Alderman W.S. Vosper, who was local secretary of the National Union of Railwaymen, suggested that figures given by British Railways of people travelling on the Yeovil to Taunton line were incorrect, but said that he was refused permission to divulge the true position!

Yeovil-Taunton was a cross-country branch line linking two important towns, and had the benefits of providing useful connections at both ends for through passengers. It was estimated that most trains carried between 30 and 40 passengers (and around 60 during busy periods), whilst on Saturday mornings each train often conveyed between 100 and 150 passengers into Taunton, many of them returning later in the day.

There being no Sunday service the final trains ran on Saturday 13th June. Whether by accident or design, the motive power provided on the day represented the principal classes that had hauled branch trains over the past 40 years. Along with the many local people who made their final journey or came to view the branch passing into history were many railway enthusiasts from around the country who travelled to photograph and ride on yet another branch line before closure.

At 7.50 pm the final departure took place from Yeovil Pen Mill, the train hauled by '41XX' 2-6-2 tank No. 4131 of Taunton Shed with driver Douglas Dominey and fireman Alan Merchant and Yeovil-based guard Charles Rodber. Just before departure a group of enthusiasts placed a wreath on the locomotive, inscribed 'In Memory of the Durston-Yeovil branch of the Bristol & Exeter Railway - born October 1853 - murdered 13th June, 1964 - gone but not forgotten'. The train was crowded with passengers standing in the corridors. Aboard were 30 children from Montacute Sunday School returning from their annual outing to Weymouth, and it was indeed an outing for them to remember. Upon arrival at Athelney the train awaited the arrival of the 8.20 pm Taunton-Yeovil service, which was to be the last passenger train to travel over the branch hauled by No. 4593 of Yeovil Shed driven by Sidney Sprague with fireman Alan Strode, the guard was Percy Webber of Taunton. As the train pulled into the station notices were to be seen pasted on the carriage windows reading, 'Marples must go!' and 'Wanted for murder, Dr Beeching, alias The Axe'. Another message was 'The end is near, Gone but not forgotten - down with Beeching' and one window exhibited a drawing of an official hanging from a gallows.

There then followed a mock funeral scene as four railway employees, Messrs Clifford Miller, Arthur Miller, Leslie Riley, and Clarence Elsbury, carried a coffin with a wreath upon it over the level crossing and placed it in the guard's van of the Yeovil-bound train. They were assisted by other employees, Reginald Haberfield and porter Clifford Miller who was wearing a frock coat and top hat!

After the two guards had exchanged trains to enable them to return to their home stations the branch trains departed from Athelney for the last time. As the last train headed towards Yeovil crowds of people waited at vantage points to

The exterior of Yeovil Town in May 1963, with modern cars parked outside. Note the British Railways sign, and the refreshment room sign, above which is one of the two roof skylights installed in 1918 when that part of the building was used as the parcels office.   *C.L. Caddy*

The exterior of Yeovil Pen Mill station viewed from the approach road in 1969, many of the features of the original stone building having changed little over the years. In the left background a single deck bus of Wakes Services waits to transport passengers to Yeovil Junction.   *Author*

Timekeeping had deteriorated even before the final singling of the line, but when this was completed locomotive failures were to add to the problems of operating over single line sections, the whole situation becoming more complicated by problems with the new signalling equipment. On 11th June 'Warship' No. D824 *Highflyer* arrived at Yeovil Junction 120 minutes late after difficulties with an up train. The situation was not improved on 19th June with the derailment of the down newspaper train near Sherborne causing diversions via Yeovil Pen Mill to Westbury and reversal before proceeding to Salisbury.

Throughout the summer and into autumn the service was subject to severe late running. From 2nd October the former down track between Sherborne and Yeovil Junction was reinstated although timekeeping remained poor. At a public meeting held in Exeter on 16th October the acting divisional manager from Bristol stated that 'the punctuality on the Exeter-Salisbury line is improving', but, hoist by his own petard, the 5 pm from Waterloo arrived at Exeter that night 45 minutes late headed by a defective 'Warship' class aptly named *Eclipse*!

Drastic alterations had also taken place on the Wilts, Somerset & Weymouth line, the severe reduction of traffic had allowed it to be converted to single line between Castle Cary and Dorchester West, with passing loops at Yeovil Pen Mill and Maiden Newton. The first section converted was Castle Cary to Yeovil Pen Mill on 12th May, 1968, the section to Maiden Newton following on the 26th and the remaining section to Dorchester West on 9th June. These alterations coincided with the withdrawal of the Yeovil Pen Mill-Yeovil Junction shuttle service after Saturday 4th May, thus ending the passenger link between the two remaining stations.

From the following Monday Hendford goods yard and the remaining section of line from Pen Mill closed. Yeovil's fortunes as a railway centre were at their lowest. Already track had been removed from Yeovil Town leaving only a single line to Hendford and a siding into the engine shed, these were shortly to be removed, the site lying derelict until purchased by Yeovil Borough Council on 30th March, 1971 for redevelopment; demolished in 1973, the major part became a car park with associated road works.

The closure of Hendford effectively ended the handling of assorted goods traffic at Yeovil. The goods concentration scheme where deliveries were made from major railheads quickly lost favour and the incorporation of the greater part of the railways' vehicle fleet into National Carriers Ltd, part of the road-biased National Freight Corporation, from 1st January, 1969 saw the gradual end of the goods sundries traffic.

Strangely Yeovil Pen Mill yard never officially closed. Although the goods shed closed many years ago the sidings on the down side were still handling wagon load traffic in late 1978 and in January 1999 a consignment of fertilizer was unloaded, whilst car carriers were unloaded at Yeovil Junction during 1985 for local dealers Abbey Hill. Parcels sent by passenger train continued, branded as 'Rail Express Parcels'. This again was phased out in 1981 leaving the prestige 'Red Star' parcels service until this in turn ceased, it becoming impossible to send a parcel by train! The parcels office at Pen Mill became a snack bar.

Towards the end '14XX' 0-4-2 tank No. 1442 shunts wagons at Hendford goods yard. After
withdrawal No. 1442 became a static exhibit alongside a main road in Tiverton. Today she
stands in a specially constructed hall in Tiverton Town museum.   *Author*

Hendford goods shed after closure of the yard. This structure constructed in 1900 quickly
proved insufficient for the needs of the district and the extension in the foreground had to be
added.   *Author*

Class '47' No. 47151 waits to depart from Yeovil Pen Mill from the up platform with a Bristol-Weymouth train on 7th August, 1974, this movement being allowed by the bi-directional signalling at the station. The hut shown on the right houses the auxiliary key token instruments for both the Yeovil Junction and Maiden Newton single line sections. *Author*

On the evening of 1st July, 1976 D1021 *Western Cavalier* passes Yeovil Junction with the Westbury-Exeter Central cement train. The train having proceeded via the single line from Yeovil Pen Mill the first section of which consists of the former up Weymouth line. *Author*

Class '50' No. 50032 *Courageous* passes Yeovil Junction signal box with a down Waterloo-Exeter train on 17th April, 1984.   *Author*

During engineering work on the GWR main line Western Region trains are often diverted via the Southern line between Exeter and Yeovil Junction, gaining their normal route again at Castle Cary. In this busy scene at Yeovil Pen Mill on 30th March, 1985 an up IC125 passes through the up platform while a class '50' waits to proceed to Yeovil Junction from the down platform. A dmu has been shunted into a siding to allow these moves.   *C.L. Caddy*

service between Bridport and Maiden Newton suffering a rapidly declining trade. The Bristol-Weymouth Line Development Group was formed in 1980, a voluntary organisation whose stated aims were: to increase patronage of the line, to provide an adequate service for all stops, to improve co-operation with other lines and other transport in the area, to encourage County Council and District Council participation; to deter any future cuts in the service, and to increase the lines potential for freight. However, little else was heard of this organisation which seems to have disappeared from the scene.

Following the re-routing of the Channel Islands boat train via the Southern route Yeovil passengers were devoid of a direct service to Weymouth Quay, having to make do with a connecting bus from Weymouth station. During the 1983 and 1984 seasons a Bristol-Weymouth dmu service was extended to Weymouth Quay once again giving a direct boat connection from the Western line, until insufficient passengers caused its withdrawal.

In March 1983 - 20 years after Beeching - the Serpell Report again put the future of many railways in doubt, Serpell recommending closing 84 per cent of the remaining network. After Beeching this scheme was 'political dynamite' and was never pursued, but if it had been what hope would there have been for either of Yeovil's railways? Options A, B, and C3 of the Report would have left no railways at or near Yeovil or indeed in any other part of the West Country, option C1 removed the Yeovil-Dorchester section, C2 also removing the Castle Cary-Yeovil section. Again in 1987 the British Railways Board devised a list of closure proposals including eight West Country branches!

The deteriorating service caused the setting up of a local gingerbread group following a meeting of interested parties at the White Horse Inn, Yeovil, in the autumn of 1983. The Yeovil & District Rail Action Group (YADRAG) was formed as a rail group with the aim of maintaining and improving the current rail services and protecting the rights of rail passengers. Founder members included the newly elected constituency MP, the Rt Hon. Paddy Ashdown who became leader of the Liberal Democrats. Originally the group consisted of individual members and initially concentrated on Yeovil's two stations and services. However, involvement with other organisations of a like kind and various councils and groups led eventually to 22 corporate members being added to the individual memberships which averaged 70.

On 16th May, 1983 the second station reopening occurred at the western end of the Waterloo line when Pinhoe was reinstated, to be followed by Templecombe on 3rd October, the latter after a long-fought campaign since 1975.

During 1983-1985, only 65-70 per cent of trains over the line ran to time or up to five minutes late, and the reliability of the class '50s' was causing concern. When running well, there was no problem with maintaining scheduled timings, but failures were increasing. The possibility of using class '47/4s' was examined but rejected, it being decided that the class '50s' would remain until High Speed Trains ('IC125s') became available following the electrification of the East Coast Main Line. IC125s were no strangers to the Salisbury-Exeter line. The first recorded visit was in October 1980 and on 24th March, 1986 No. 43002 *Top of the Pops* worked a special to Gillingham conveying VIPs for the inauguration of the new passing loop at Tisbury. IC125s were often to be seen between Yeovil

Class '33' No. 33035 departs from Yeovil Junction with an Exeter train. To the right an
engineer's train stands on the former down through line. On the left are the station
master's house and the original goods shed, the latter being converted into a garage.
Author

Junction and Exeter when that section was used as a diversionary route
between Castle Cary and Exeter for Western Region trains.

The decision to set up five British Rail business sectors resulted in yet another
change on 10th June, 1986 when the Salisbury-Exeter line became part of the
newly formed Network SouthEast. The new sector covered 2,500 route miles
from Kings Lynn and Harwich in the East, to a northern boundary around
Banbury, Northampton, Bedford, and Huntingdon, and embracing the entire
South East of England to include Weymouth in the South West and the
Salisbury-Exeter line to Exeter in the West.

Over the years there had been various suggestions for improving the
interchange facilities between Pen Mill and Yeovil Junction - particularly since
the demise of the shuttle service. The provision of a platform on the
Weymouth line at or near the point where it passes under the Southern line,
with a footpath leading to Yeovil Junction has been suggested but for various
reasons not proceeded with. A report by the Dorset County Council Surveyor
to the Council and the Somerset County Council in August 1987 included the
following points:

   British Rail sees potential for reducing the costs of staff and facilities in Yeovil by
having one staffed station at Yeovil instead of two. They also consider the potential
revenue would accrue if connectional facilities were improved. The key area of lost
business is from Weymouth to the West of England. A 'point of sale' for rail travel in
Yeovil town centre is also proposed.
   Signalling will have to be replaced at Yeovil Pen Mill in the very near future, and at
Yeovil Junction in the next 5-7 years. British Rail after exploring many options,
therefore seem to favour a plan, which will divert the Bristol-Weymouth rail service via
Yeovil Junction. This will be achieved by laying a new curve of railway track from

which included a 51 ft brake third of 1905, converted in 1915 for service in the London area. In 1924, especially for the Yeovil service, two compartments were removed to enlarge the luggage space in the guard's van, and in this form it remained until withdrawn in April 1940.Various sets were employed over the years, one of the 'Gate Sets' being in service during 1935 whilst in the late 1940s set No. 659 - consisting of former South Eastern & Chatham Railway stock and still retaining its 'Birdcage' guard's lookout - was employed.

The early 1950s saw the arrival of set No. 383, reconstructed in October 1948 from an LSWR two-coach Ironclad set consisting of 57 ft brake composite No. 6562 and brake third No. 3211. In the conversion the toilets in both coaches were made into coupé compartments with six seats! The brake third had an extra compartment added in the luggage space and both brake ends were formed into driving ends.

The summer of 1959 saw the return of the sole surviving 'Gate Set', No. 373, formed by 56 ft brake third No. 4303 and 56 ft trailer third No. 4265. Its stay at Yeovil was brief, moving on within a year. Withdrawn in October 1960 it was considered for official preservation; unfortunately it was eventually condemned and broken up.

The GWR type auto-coaches were constructed in June 1954 as lot 1766 and consisted of 10 vehicles. Generally following GWR design, they were 63 ft long and flush sided, having 70 motorbus type seats and four folding seats in the luggage space. During the period of their stay four of the batch worked at Yeovil - Nos. 235, 236, 238 and 240. Of these, Nos. 238 and 240 passed into preservation with the Dart Valley Railway at Buckfastleigh. No. 238 later moved to the Paignton & Dartmouth Steam Railway and now named *Charlotte* works as an ordinary coach on service trains. No. 240 remains at Buckfastleigh (now the South Devon Railway) and at the time of writing remains a long-term restoration project.

The nature of push-pull trains called for special regulations which were clearly set out in the 1921 LSWR book of Rules and Regulations, for instance:

> When a push and pull train is run with the engine at the rear, the guard must ride with the engine driver in the leading brake compartment, and in the event of the train's failure in a section with the engine at the rear, the guard will walk forward for the assisting engine and the fireman walk back to protect the train.

Later certain push-pull trains including those between Yeovil Junction-Yeovil Town were allowed to operate without a guard, the 1934 Southern Railway Appendix again giving clear instructions as to their operation:

> When pull and push trains are working without a guard between the under mentioned points, and the engine is propelling, an exchange of bell signals, viz., two rings, must be made between the driver and fireman 100yds from Yeovil Town up home signal and 100yds from Yeovil Junction down home signal. In the absence of a bell signal from the driver the fireman must be prepared to bring the train to a stand at the signal, level crossing, or station as the case may be.
>
> A porter will accompany the train between Yeovil Junction and Yeovil Town when necessary for the purpose of giving assistance with the loading of parcels, luggage and mails. He must ride in the brake compartment and take charge of and sort mails, parcels and luggage. He will undertake no responsibility appertaining to the actual running of the train.

Chapter Fifteen

Associated Bus Services

After the horse buses that had plied between the various hotels and the stations several of these proprietors continued with motor vehicles, their operation being more regulated following the 1930 Road Traffic Act. Mr F. W. Cole of the Three Choughs Hotel operated between Yeovil Pen Mill and Town Railway stations and any point in the Borough daily. 'The vehicle operating the service shall bear in a conspicuous position a sign stating Station Bus - Minimum fare 6d.' In later years it was operated in conjunction with A. J. Croft of the Mermaid Hotel and acquired by him early in 1937 when Cole left the Three Choughs.

Croft, who also ran between the Yeovil railway stations and town (passengers only), operated a Ford seven-seat bus after 1924, replaced by a Chevrolet in 1928, his service continuing until World War II.

However, with the 1920s came a new threat to the railways in the form of the motor bus. Until then the local carters had provided a complementary service between the villages and towns making a connection with the railway for the cartage of goods, parcels and the occasional passenger, but this was to change as the motor bus commenced to cover a much wider area and offer an alternative form of transport, usually taking passengers nearer to their actual destination than the railway station.

The National Omnibus & Transport Company was rapidly expanding westwards from London and the eastern counties. On 5th July, 1920 it took over the service operated by Mr Bates who, trading as White Bros and Bates, operated between South Petherton and Yeovil. Applying successfully to Yeovil Council for licences, services were quickly commenced between Yeovil, Martock and Bower Hinton, Yeovil and Crewkerne, and Yeovil to Sherborne and Milborne Port. The *Western Gazette* referred to the new services with a headline 'Ousting the Trains', saying how convenient the service would be and doing away with much of the uncertainty and inconvenience met with on the railways. The fares were also more moderate than those in force on the railways.

At first the buses were kept at a site near Pen Mill station with one vehicle out-stationed at Milborne Port, but in August 1921 National acquired the former Petter's Nautilus Works in Reckleford, Yeovil, as a garage - and it remains so until the present day. In the same year a Yeovil-Somerton-Langport-Taunton service was commenced, and National's foothold was further strengthed in 1921 when, following the closure of the Taunton electric tramway, it became possible to establish a town service to give them a base for further rural expansion. The year 1922 saw the commencement of a Yeovil Pen Mill-Sparkford-Castle Cary-Shepton Mallet service.

During 1923 the services of W. Pennell King of Crewkerne who ran to Yeovil were acquired. The Golden Age of the railways had come to an end, their monopoly broken for both passenger and goods traffic as the motor vehicle developed during the 1920s. However, the introduction of a group of town services during 1928 serving both Yeovil Town and Pen Mill stations (particularly the latter) were of advantage to rail travellers. 1929 saw the introduction of what was described as a service in partnership with the railways. Operating between Milborne Port and Wincanton via Templecombe station this came at a time when the National Omnibus & Transport Company was split into three, the Yeovil area becoming part of the new Southern National of which the Railways had a 51 per cent share, and to a degree gained some control over its future expansion.

Southern National also began to acquire various independent operators in the area to strengthen its position. In November 1932 Wincanton Motor Services was taken over. They had commenced in 1920 with a Wincanton to Yeovil service via Sparkford on Monday, Wednesday, Friday, and Saturdays. By 1931 they operated a Friday-only service from Wincanton to Yeovil via Bratton Seymour and North Cadbury, and a Monday service from Wincanton to Yeovil via Templecombe and Henstridge. They also ran services to Gillingham, Salisbury and Frome.

In 1933 the Bradford Abbas Bus Service owned by Mrs E.E. Ellwood was acquired, running into Yeovil via Nether Compton and Over Compton twice daily on Mondays, Wednesdays and Fridays and three times on Saturdays. Two further small operators were acquired during 1935. A.E. Bath of Corscombe, who had commenced operations during 1922 using a small Reo vehicle ran into Yeovil via Halstock, Sutton Bingham and East Coker; whilst W.H. Parker of Barton St David, trading as 'One Man Band', was by 1931 running a service from Street to Yeovil via Barton St David and Somerton and also ran into Glastonbury. During World War II the service was transferred to Bristol Tramways, thus giving them their most southerly route which is still run by their successor company, First Bus.

The year 1936 saw the acquisition of Sullys Services of Horton, Ilminster. They had been a major competitor to both the railway and Western/Southern National between Taunton, Chard, Axminster and Lyme Regis, and they also operated a service between Ilminster and Yeovil via Shepton Beauchamp and Martock.

Whereas Sullys Services was successful and a threat to Southern National, Three Counties Motors Ltd of Wincanton failed. Originally operating from Mere with a service to Yeovil via Wincanton, Stalbridge and Stourton Caundle, further applications to operate services into Yeovil were refused by the Traffic Commissioners in 1931, the business going into liquidation during 1934.

It was not only the local services of the railway that were open to competition from the expanding bus services. The long distance coach had arrived and Yeovil, being a cross roads of trunk routes, was suitably served. By the summer of 1935 the following Royal Blue Routes passed through the town: London-Exeter-Paignton-Plymouth; London-Taunton-Minehead-Barnstaple-Lynton, or Bideford-Bude; Bournemouth-Taunton-Weston-super-Mare; and London-Cornwall services. Associated Motorways operated from Cheltenham to Bath-Shepton Mallet-Yeovil and Weymouth, and in the summer of 1938 introduced a Bristol-Yeovil-Bridport service. These routes, with later improvements gave the public a wide choice of destinations.

Bird Bros (Transport) Ltd of Woodlands Garage, Yeovil was a well-founded business dating back to 1919 who by 1937 were operating 24 lorries and 6 coaches. The latter were employed on tours, private hire, and more-importantly a group of summer weekend holiday express services to Southsea, Bournemouth, Weymouth and Torquay. Owing to several of these being in competition with Royal Blue, Southern National purchased the coaching side of the business on 12th April, 1937, the operations being integrated into the Royal Blue and Southern National services.

Although Southern National had taken over a number of smaller independent operators, there were three which survived and flourished to become a major part of the local transport network. In November 1927 Thomas Hutchings of South Petherton started a daily service to Yeovil Pen Mill station via Stoke sub Hamdon and Montacute. To this he added a route from Chiselborough through Stoke sub Hamdon (this being extended to West Chinnock and later Crewkerne). In addition some journeys served Westland's at work times. In May 1928 Alfred Cornelius, who was landlord of the Royal Oak at Barrington, commenced a service from Shepton Beauchamp to Taunton via Curry Rivel, later adding a second route from Ilminster to Yeovil via Barrington, Shepton Beauchamp, Kingsbury Episcopi, Ash and Tintinhull.

On 31st May, 1934 the two businesses were combined to form Hutchings & Cornelius, the two owners being joined as Directors by Stanley Vincent, a Yeovil garage proprietor. One peculiarity that survived to the end was that the two depots were virtually separate concerns, Barrington as 'Cornelius's' covering the Taunton runs, and South Petherton as 'Hutchings' operating to Yeovil.

Hutchings had commenced operations with a Chevrolet and a Thornycroft, whilst Cornelius had a Chevrolet, Thornycroft and Dennis. Both owners liked Thornycroft vehicles, the combined fleet consisting of eight such vehicles - four from each owner - and a Dennis from Cornelius. The fleet carried the black and cream livery formerly used by Cornelius, this changing to light blue with grey lining around 1943. Various second-hand vehicles were acquired, particularly during the war years. In 1950 MYA 391 and MYA 816, two Jensen chassis with Sparshatt B40F bodies, were acquired (a very rare breed!) and in 1953 the first double-deck joined the fleet in the form of former Huddersfield Corporation No. 204 Daimler CW6A with a Brush 55-seat lowbridge body and was employed on the Yeovil route.

Over the years Vincent had obtained more shares in the business and in 1954 the Vincent family became the sole owners, the fleet livery being changed to red and cream. Between 1954 and 1958 seven Dennis UF Lancets were purchased and in 1958, 623 BYA a Dennis Lowline, East Lancs-bodied LD68R double-deck joined the fleet. In 1961 the fleet strength stood at 21 vehicles. The company was the first outside the National Bus Company to purchase two Bristol LH chassis and later the first Bristol VRT supplied to an independent operator, RYA 600L.

Although there was strong competition from Southern National 'H&C' (as they were known) were very popular with local people and frequently duplicates (often more than one) were required on both routes. As with other operators, the firm saw a decline in passengers from the late 1960s onwards and faced with decreased revenue and rising operating costs, fares were increased and services reduced. The owners found it increasingly difficult to obtain a reasonable return on capital compared with what was achievable within the motor trade and following a demand for a rise in drivers' wages the Vincent family decided to close the business, services ceasing after 31st May, 1979. Thus after 45 years H&C disappeared from the local scene, Western National, Safeway's, and Brutonian providing replacement services.

Another publican, Gilbert Gunn of South Petherton, together with his son Herbert, who after an apprenticeship with Westland's was employed by the National Omnibus Company at Yeovil until 1928, set up a family business to be known as 'Safeway'. This used a Dennis G type bus operating a service between Hinton St George, Crewkerne, and Yeovil, the first and last journeys running to and from their base at South Petherton.

Competition was fierce as National endeavoured to run their former employee off the road, but he persevered and expanded the business with Herbert's sister Veronica joining to help. Herbert carried out the maintenance work, whilst Veronica did the office work and often conducted with Herbert driving. The mainstay of the business remained the main bus route and in post-war years a workmen's service to and from Westland's was started. Private hire work was expanded after Veronica persuaded her brother to acquire Ernest Giles 'Venture Coaches' of South Petherton and his tours programme was extended.

Veronica Gunn was to become one of the best known, and most independent of, operators in the West Country. During the 1960s she came into prominence when she refused to increase fares to come into line with Southern National, believing that it would drive passengers away. She even appeared on television and finally won the day.

Following the withdrawal of H&C in 1979, Safeway took over their South Petherton, Crewkerne and Ilminster to Yeovil routes, excursions and a school contract and soon after a run to Taunton. After deregulation there was a challenge from Kingston Coaches of Yeovil (Yeovilian) who cut fares, but Miss Gunn refused to follow suit and there were reports of duplication, racing, etc. Eventually the newcomers conceded defeat and withdrew. Her brother having pre-deceased her, Miss Veronica Gunn MBE continued to run the business until suffering a stroke in 1999. She died in the August of that year, aged 91, the business being continued by her nephew, Vernon.

During its time South Petherton must go down in history as having had three bus companies based in a village with a population of only around 2,500 for - as well as H&C and Safeway's - Southern National maintained a depot within the village housed in a former hall.

The third pre-war survivor was Wakes Services of Sparkford. Reginald Wake, the son of a GWR employee, commenced business at South Barrow in February 1930 with a second-hand Chevrolet operating market day services to Glastonbury on Tuesdays, Shepton Mallet on Fridays and Yeovil on Saturdays. During the 1930s a Castle Cary-Yeovil service was started which was more convenient than the trains, as it actually dropped passengers off in the centre of Yeovil and not at Pen Mill which was to the east side of the town.

The beginning of motor bus competition. Herbert Gunn stands alongside YD 1728, a Dennis Dart fitted with a Strachan B20F body. New to Gunn (Safeway Services) on 12th March, 1931, the vehicle passed to Alexander (Comfy Coaches), Horsham, during 1937 and was disposed of in February 1939. *Roger Grimley Collection*

After 1948 the station forecourt at Yeovil Town became an *ad hoc* coach station, the station buffet providing refreshment facilities. Many coaches of the Royal Blue and Associated Motorways network with West Country destinations made connections, although few passengers transferred from the trains! Lined up on 4th June, 1955 are, *from left to right*: Western National Bristol 'LL6B' No. 1301, LTA 739; Greenslades AEC 'Regal III' KFJ 614; Devon General (Grey Cars) AEC 'Regal IV' NUO 685; AEC 'Regal III', LTA 631 and LTA 634. The three latter coaches were later acquired by Greenslades. *G.M. Stubbs*

The fact that Reginald's father was employed by the railway proved a difficulty when a new vehicle was purchased in April 1934 from Dunn's Motors of Taunton (himself also a bus operator). Messrs Dunn explained to the hire purchase company that, 'you will observe that Mr Wake, senior, is a railwayman and it is not in his interests to sign this agreement owing to his son being in opposition to the railway'. In the circumstances the hire purchase company accepted Dunn's undertaking to repurchase in place of the parent's guarantee. Ironically a quote by the GWR to deliver the new motor from Hendon to Sparkford at station - to - station rate was 37s. 11d. per ton for motorcars on their own wheels exceeding 30 cwt!

The business moved to Sparkford in 1940 where a motor garage was taken over, the bus and coach side of the business expanding considerably during the war when many vehicles were purchased to convey construction workers engaged in building airfields and military bases in the area. Following the war servicemen's weekend leave services were operated to London and the South Coast, whilst the Yeovil-Castle Cary service was extended to Shepton Mallet and operated daily. Two AEC Regent double-deckers, both with L54R Reading bodies - LYA 449 and LYB 113, were purchased in 1949 for the service, being joined in 1960 by a second-hand Bristol K6A ECW, KHU 623, formerly Bristol Omnibus No. L4102. By 1953 the fleet consisted of 15 vehicles of AEC, Bedford, Commer and Dennis manufacture.

During 1956 the business of 'English Rose Coaches' (Chinn) of Wincanton was acquired, giving Wakes a second base and a network of rural services based in that town. In 1958 Grosvenor Coaches of Shaftesbury was purchased together with the licence for excursions from the town. By the early 1960s the forces' leave services had ceased. Turning their attention to the forthcoming railway closures following the Beeching report, two Bedford buses were purchased for an intended railway replacement service between Blandford and Glastonbury or Midsomer Norton due to commence on 3rd January, 1966. However, the application was withdrawn when the closure of the Somerset & Dorset Railway was delayed.

From 6th May, 1968 Wakes, following withdrawal of the shuttle service, commenced a daily service between Yeovil Junction and Pen Mill stations - a service that was to cause much controversy over the years and problems for various operators. Generally as with other operators, passenger numbers declined from the 1960s and the firm later relied heavily on subsidy and County Council-tendered work. By this time Dennis and Michael Wake had inherited the business from their father and they sold it to Hulbert of Yeovil (now South West Coaches) on 10th January, 2000, the well known Sparkford site having been closed.

From the south, two rural Dorset operators, Legg's of Evershot and Pearce of Cattistock, served Yeovil. Frank Legg had commenced a motorised carriers service in August 1920 between Evershot and Yeovil on Mondays and Fridays, and southwards from Evershot to Dorchester on Wednesday and Saturdays, serving Maiden Newton, Frampton, Grimstone and Stratton *en route*, thus creating the first serious opposition to the railway along the Yeovil-Weymouth line. Legg later expanded into the haulage business, in particular livestock, abstracting more trade from the railway.

LYA 449 one of two AEC 'Regents' with Reading L54R bodies purchased in 1949 by Wakes Services, seen here parked at the company's Sparkford garage on 3rd October, 1965. The destination blind displays 'Castle Cary, via Marston Magna and Sparkford' showing that the vehicle was operating the route from Yeovil parallel to the railway.   *C.L. Caddy*

MYA 516, one of two Jensen single-deck vehicles operated by Hutchings & Cornelius, the rare chassis being complimented by a B40F Sparshatt body. A close examination of the front-end reveals that the driver was in a sealed off cab, and the sliding door to the passenger compartment was across the front in line with the front bulkhead.   *R.B. Gossling Collection*

Southern National No. 1619, a Bristol LWL6B, ECW B39F, returns to the garage from Yeovil Pen Mill station after working a 7A service between Crewkerne and Yeovil Pen Mill station. Assuming the train and bus connections were reasonable, this gave a 45 minute bus journey, quicker than the three train changes!   *P. Trevaskis*

The bus side of the business was sold in November 1954 to Pearce of Cattistock who also operated over part of the same route to Dorchester. Albert Pearce had purchased the coal delivery and carriers business of Percy Shorto in 1918. Purchasing his first motor vehicle in 1923, he continued the Dorchester service and commenced a service to Yeovil on Fridays and alternate Mondays. The Yeovil service ceased in the late 1920s but the Dorchester and other services expanded.

Meanwhile, following World War II Cyril Darch, who ran a cycle and wireless shop, taxi service, and petrol pumps at Martock, purchased a coach in 1948 and with his son-in-law commenced private hire and contract work. In 1960 the goodwill and tours licences of Barlow Phillips, a Yeovil coach operator and haulier ,were acquired.

In 1972 Darch & Willcox joined forces with Pearce of Cattistock to form Pearce Darch & Willcox, and again the business expanded, but unfortunately following deregulation and the loss of contracts and tendered services Cattistock garage was closed concentrating the business at Martock. With other firms submitting very low tenders the business was sold to the Cawlett Group on 1st April, 1990.

The outbreak of World War II reduced bus services as fuel rationing began to take effect and both large and small operators struggled to provide a service. Later both the Royal Blue and Associated Motorways coach services were withdrawn, these gradually returning for the 1947 season. Slowly after the war services returned to normal. As in stage coach days Yeovil was a convenient place for passengers to take a refreshment break, but owing to difficulties in finding suitable accommodation within the town in December 1947 negotiations were concluded with both the GWR and SR to allow Royal Blue coaches to use the Yeovil Town refreshment rooms. Thus at certain times of day, and on Saturdays in particular, the station approach road resembled a coach station. The following year the nationalisation of the railways and the acquisition of the Tilling Group of bus companies was to bring the two still closer together. It was not until the building of the new bus station in Earle Street that the buses and coaches were to leave the station approach. Although it had been an *ad hoc* arrangement it had served well! Many of the longer distance bus services had also commenced from Station Road.

There was to be no further acquisition of operators until October 1953 when the business of Wintle, of Bower Hinton, was taken over by Southern National. The six vehicle fleet was employed on a daily service between Bower Hinton and Yeovil via Ash and Tintinhull, a works contract and excursions and tours. The business had commenced in 1922 as Wintle & Murray using a primitive vehicle with open windows over which canvas curtains could be dropped. Joseph Wintle later bought out his partner, and continued the service until he sold out to Southern National.

The next change of any significance was to follow the 1968 Transport Act, which allowed the creation of the National Bus Company (NBC) to take over the bus interests of the Transport Holding Company (THC) from 1st January, 1969. Southern National, a former member of the Tilling Group, which had been absorbed into the THC, automatically became a unit of the newly formed NBC. It was the beginning of a new era of bus operation.

On 8th June, 1969 there was a complete renumbering of Southern National routes into the 400 series, but in January 1970 Southern National ceased to exist as a separate operation, being absorbed into the larger Western National. From 1972 the fleet started to lose its familiar Tilling green livery in favour of the new NBC leaf green.

During this period there was a marked decline in the use of public transport and many cuts were made to services. There were also political changes afoot, and by the early 1980s the Government wanted to divest itself of the bus industry, so it then became policy to break the companies up into smaller units to make them attractive for privatisation. Thus Western National was split on 1st January, 1984 and Southern National was reborn with main depots at Weymouth, Yeovil, and Taunton - where a head office was established.

The 1985 Transport Act, which came into force on 26th October, 1986, freed bus services from the Road Service Licensing system, and they were therefore open to competition. More importantly, no longer was an operator protected once he obtained a licence for a route, and the strict safeguards covering timetables and fares were swept aside. The road was open to all comers providing they held an operator's licence and registered the route with the authorities. It was open season for all!

In Yeovil there was one major development. G. Coleman, who traded as 'Kingston Coaches' and adopted the fleet name 'Yeovilian', commenced three routes to Crewkerne on 11th January, 1988 (services 001, 002 and 003). The first two were in competition with Safeway's, the 002 via Montacute, whilst 003 in competition with Southern National ran via Martock. On the latter route Southern National responded aggressively with increased frequencies and by reducing fares by over 50 per cent, Yeovilian withdrew in the March. Safeway's provided good competition which caused the 002 to cease in the spring of 1989, although the 001 (with many journeys cut back to Merriott) survived until the end of the company's operations on 16th February, 1990.

Yeovilian also attempted two town services, 010 to the Eliotts Drive area commencing on 14th March, 1988, and 030 to St Johns Road on 19th May. But strong competition from Southern National and a driver shortage by Yeovilian caused both services to fade away in mid-September 1988, since which date all services in the area have been provided by the previously established operators.

During the above period the sale of constituent companies of the NBC went ahead. Southern National, the 69th to be sold, was purchased by its management on 29th March, 1988, a holding company, Cawlett Ltd, being formed. The Cawlett group was itself acquired by First Bus on 8th April, 1999 and, as with most large concerns where image is all-important, Southern National became 'First Southern National'. This was taken further from November 2001 when the fleet name was changed to just 'First', thus after 81 years 'National's' association with the Yeovil area had ended.

The Yeovil Junction Shuttle Bus

Following the withdrawal of the railway shuttle service between Yeovil Pen Mill and Yeovil Junction the shuttle bus commenced on 6th May, 1968, operated by Wakes of Sparkford, with a daily service including Sundays. Found not to be a viable proposition, Wakes withdrew after 30th June, 1972, from which time there was no connecting service, much to the advantage of local taxi drivers!

This state of affairs also persuaded those who were able to travel by bus to use Sherborne as their rail-head (a policy mooted by British Rail in 1964). It was not until 14th May, 1979 that a further attempt was made to provide a bus link between the two stations, this time operated by G. Coleman, trading as 'Kingston Coaches', operating a service via the town centre, Hendford Hill, the Quicksilver Mail, and Two Tower Lane. This again was ran seven days a week; although its life was short and it was withdrawn early that July owing to fuel shortages!

Again the taxi drivers enjoyed a monopoly until 1984 when the matter was taken up by both Dorset and Somerset County Councils. The provision of a bus link was a Dorset County Council initiative with the County Council being the tendering authority, the subsidy cost being shared between Dorset County Council, Somerset County Council and British Rail. The service commenced on 4th June, 1984 with Southern National operating it as service No. 480, running from Pen Mill via the car park on the site of the former Town station then via Newton Road to Yeovil Junction. During the afternoons two services ran to Yetminster station as there was insufficient time for the return to Pen Mill. The service was altered from 3rd June, 1985 when Yeovil bus station became the town pick up point instead of the old station car park.

On deregulation the route was re-tendered and Air Camelot, a newly formed company based on the former Brutonian Bus Company, which it had acquired, took over the operation from the 27th October, 1986. Commencing on 5th October, 1987 outward services to the junction incorporated a double run to Stoford. However, the new operator failed to make an impact on local service work and from 28th March, 1988 the service reverted to Southern National as service No 80 and, without the Stoford extension, continued to operate until 31st March, 1995. Throughout that period the route had been equally subsidised by the two County Councils and British Rail, but following a local government boundary review which moved Yeovil Junction out of Dorset into Somerset, Dorset County Council withdrew its share of the subsidy causing the service to be withdrawn after 27th May, 1995. Again there was no service until 1st July when Southern National, with Somerset County Council, recommenced it with South West Trains providing some new funding. As it was considered the section between the bus station and Pen Mill was sufficiently well covered by other services the decision was taken to provide only a link between the bus station and Yeovil Junction, now numbered 980.

Throughout its history the service has been dogged with problems, not assisted by the poor road access to Yeovil Junction and the difficulty of making as many connections as possible with a single vehicle. The times of trains at Pen Mill and those at Yeovil Junction did not lend themselves well to a one-vehicle operation, but expanding the service to two vehicles has not been an option in view of the relatively small number of passengers carried.

Southern National minibus No. 352, C914 GYD a 1986 Ford 'Transit' with a Dormobile B16F body, waits to depart from Yeovil Junction for the town. The minibus was introduced as the answer to ailing services and, although very reliable mechanically, had little to commend them for passenger comfort. Being little more than a van with seats, they were often referred to as 'bread vans'.   *B. Thirlwall*

Appendix One

Sundry Working Arrangements

Yeovil Town, being a joint station, had many complications in its operation. The Minute books for the Joint Committee appointed to oversee the working are full of disagreements over various matters, some of which are detailed in the text of this book, which ranged from serious points of responsibility, costs, and ownership down to what the 'outsider' would consider so trivial as to scarcely be worth bothering about! However, the letter of the agreements and company honour had to be seen to be satisfied.

There was the question of land purchased from the Harbin estate in 1869 and the rental due from three traders occupying part of it. The rental due in 1906-7 amounted to £2 3s. 9d., which after deductions, left the GWR with a mere 5s. 9d. Even the water for flushing the toilet at the West signal box did not escape a charge of 10s. against the GWR, and the amount of waste and signal lamp wicks used by the Joint signal boxes came under scrutiny.

During March 1908 there was correspondence concerning telephone arrangements. The telephone company had fixed 12 insulators, six on LSWR property, and six on Joint property, the Estate Agent of the GWR having agreed to the work being carried out subject to a proper proportion of the wayleave rental being brought into the Joint account. This amounted to 30s. per annum, but there was also a telephone wire running across Joint land to the office of the Direct Coal Supply Company which attracted a wayleave rental of 5s. per annum.

Other oddities included the refreshment room at Yeovil Town. In January 1888 Messrs Spiers & Pond took over the running for all the refreshment rooms on the LSWR for £12,500 per year - but Yeovil Town cost them an extra £100. In 1895 the refreshment room agreement was so tightly controlled as to state the prices to be charged for both food and drinks. The cost of running the refreshment rooms increased in 1909 when the yearly rental was raised to 15 per cent of the gross receipts in lieu of 10 per cent as previously - but with the same minimum rent. It is interesting to note that Yeovil Junction refreshment rooms were always operated by a private individual and were never involved in the Spiers & Pond contract.

The station had two station masters from opening, the LSWR man living at the east end of the building and the GWR at the west end. From its opening until the reduction of manpower caused by World War I the station had three sets of staff! LSWR staff and GWR staff (B&E pre-1876), under the direction of their respective station masters, attended to the business of their respective companies and the transfer of traffic from one to the other under certain conditions. There was also a 'joint' staff - a small group consisting of the signalmen at both boxes and the lamp man. All signalmen were passed to work both boxes, although appointments to the East box were usually from LSWR staff whilst the GWR appointed men for the West box. The GWR was responsible for the maintenance of the signalling and the permanent way, whilst the LSWR maintained and carried out repairs to the station buildings - including those used by the GWR.

The amount of broad and mixed gauge track at Yeovil Town is open to speculation, although the B&E/GWR only occupied the running line through the station from Pen Mill to Hendford, the short parcel bay behind the GWR platform and the two adjacent short loading dock sidings. The photograph of *Frome* at Yeovil Town in 1862 clearly shows no mixed gauge track in the yard of the engine shed.

The two private sidings at Yeovil Town deserve special mention by nature of their access. The 1934 Southern Railway Appendices outlined the details:

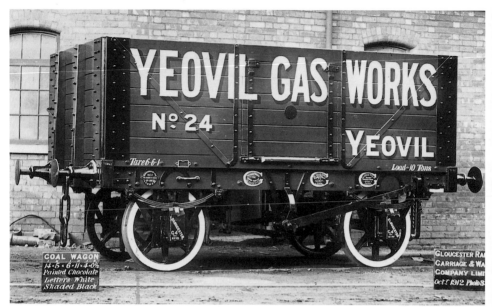

Prior to nationalisation private owner wagons were a common sight on all railways. Local wagons of particular interest included this 8-plank 10 ton example, constructed by the Gloucester Railway Carriage & Wagon Company in October 1912 for Yeovil gasworks and was painted chocolate with white lettering shaded in black.   *Author's Collection*

Also constructed by the Gloucester Company in June 1904 was this 5-plank 8 ton wagon for the Somerset Trading Company painted bright red with white lettering shaded black. Today the Somerset Trading Company is part of Bradford's, who still serve Yeovil.   *Author's Collection*

E. J. Farr & Co's Siding. - This siding forms a continuation of the siding running parallel to the cart road opposite the goods shed at Yeovil Town station and leads to Messrs E.J. Farr & Co's wool stores, access being obtained by means of a turntable situated in the goods yard.

Immediately beyond the siding gate near the company's boundary, the siding crosses a public cart road known as Dodham lane, on the opposite side of which another gate is provided across the siding, which is under the control of Messrs Farr & Coy. This gate is kept locked after business hours and the keys are kept by the traders.

Before vehicles are placed or taken from the private siding, the shunter in charge of the operation must open and secure the gate on the station side of the level crossing, and must also satisfy himself that the gate controlled by Messrs Farr & Co. is likewise open and secure. During the time wagons are actually being hauled to and from the siding, the shunter in charge must stand at the level crossing to prevent the passage of road vehicles over it until the rail vehicles have passed clear of the crossing.

Vehicles for the private siding must be placed immediately inside the gate controlled by Messrs Farr & Co. and vehicles from the siding must be accepted at that point. The responsibility for hauling vehicles to and from the point of exchange near the gate will rest with Messrs Farr & Co. and under no circumstances must the company's horses take vehicles beyond that point.

Yeovil Corporation Gas Works Siding. - Connection to this private siding is provided from one of the company's sidings by means of a turntable.

Immediately beyond the gate near the company's boundary the siding crosses the public cart road known as Dodham Lane.

The point of exchange for vehicles to and from the private siding is on the company's siding near the turntable and wagons are passed over the turntable and hauled to and from the gas works by the Corporation employees, who are responsible for the protection of road vehicles using the crossing during the time vehicles are passing to and from the siding.

The earlier 1921 LSWR Appendices paid special attention to the working of the Clifton Maybank spur in view of the 1 in 58 falling gradient towards the GWR main line.

Connections between Yeovil Junction Goods Yard Sidings and GWR Sidings at Clifton May Bank.

The points leading from the L&SW sidings to the GW line lie normally for the L&SW Siding and have to be held for movements from the siding to the GWR line.

Owing to the steep gradient falling towards the GW line, the points leading to and from that line must be kept closed and padlocked when not in use, the keys of the points at the L&SW end to be kept by the GW Co.'s checker at Clifton May Bank, and those leading from the GW line to the L&SW sidings to be kept in the custody of the L&SW station master at Yeovil Junction.

Wagons must not be pushed from the L&SW company's yard to the GW company's arrival road unless an engine is standing at the Paul's Siding end of that road, and a sufficient number of brakes have been put down on the leading wagons to control the movement over the falling gradient.

By 1934 the instructions had been amended, the principal new one being that:

The key to Paul's Siding must be kept at Clifton May Bank signal box and handed to the guard of each trip (Pen Mill to Clifton May Bank) who will be responsible for setting the points for that siding on arrival of the train and before shunting operations are commenced, and the points must remain in this position until the train is ready to return.

'2251' class 0-6-0 No. 2211 of Taunton Shed stands at Hendford on the top end of the second line from Yeovil Town on 29th May, 1954, having been shunted clear to allow a branch train to pass. Viewed from Yew Tree bridge, the original wooden structure of the halt and the oil lamp at the end of the signal box are just visible.   *G.M. Stubbs*

A steel mineral wagon stands near one of the wagon turntables in the goods yard at Yeovil Town. In the background is the goods shed, with the station buildings behind the wagons to the left.   *John Day*

Westland's Siding

With the construction of the new Westland's factory in 1913 provision was made for a private siding, the agreement with the GWR being signed on 29th March that year. It would appear that no locomotive was employed until 1920 when a Manning, Wardle saddle tank was purchased.

Like many industrial locomotives she had led a nomadic existence and exact details of her movements are lost in time. Built in August 1866 as works No. 213, she was an 'E' type 0-4-0 with cylinders of 9½ in. diameter and 14 in. stroke with 2 ft 9 in. driving wheels. When new she was delivered to Messrs Wm Moss, a contractor of Stafford, and carried the name *Stafford*. Records show that in January 1881 she was rebuilt by Manning, Wardle and given a new works number 736, passing then to Lucas & Aird (contractors), and carried the name *Boyne*. Later - at a date unspecified - Messrs P. Baker of Cardiff again rebuilt the engine.

Acquired in 1904 by Messrs Dixon & Cardus Ltd of Northam, Southampton, who were manufacturers of artificial manure, oil cake, and linseed oil, and renamed *Eva*, she shunted around the Northam Quay line until sold to Petter's in 1920. Retaining the same name she remained at Yeovil for the remainder of her working life. Although a diesel shunter arrived in 1931, *Eva* remained as a spare until broken up during 1935.

The diesel shunter was a Fowler diesel-mechanical 0-4-0 (works No. 19425). Doubtless because her owners were the manufacturers, it was fitted with a Petter's three-cylinder 'Ace' diesel engine, and the locomotive also carried the name *Ace*. In 1939 the oil engine division passed to Messrs Brush of Loughborough and *Ace* was transferred to the Leicestershire site where she remained until 1962.

The replacement at Yeovil was a second-hand 'Howard' 0-4-0 petrol-mechanical shunter built by J. & F. Howard of Bedford. Its previous history is unknown and following its arrival at Westland's it was not very successful, suffering from a number of breakdowns which resulted in the engine being replaced by one from a Fordson tractor during 1942. Its failures resulted in the hiring of engines from the GWR during the war years - including two of particular historical interest. In 1940 0-6-0 saddle tank No. 2195 *Cym Mawr* came, built in 1905 as No. 5 for the Burry Port & Gwendraeth Valley Railway. She spent many years working the Weymouth Harbour Tramway until withdrawn in March 1939. Reinstated in December 1939, she spent her time in the Bristol division until finally withdrawn in January 1953.

The second was of much greater antiquity, No. 5 *Portishead*, originally constructed by the London Brighton & South Coast Railway in June 1877 as 'A1' class 0-6-0 tank No. 43 *Gipsyhill*. She become Southern Railway No. 643 and, by then reconstructed as an 'A1X', she was sold to the Weston, Clevedon & Portishead Light Railway for £785 at the end of 1925 to become their No. 2 named *Portishead*. Taken over by the GWR in July 1940 she retained her name but became GWR No. 5 and was allocated to the Bristol Division. Her stay at Yeovil was short - 14th-19th July, 1945 - but she was allocated to Taunton between December 1948 and January 1950 and finally withdrawn in March 1954.

It would appear that the Howard either improved or was tolerated, for it remained until the closure of the siding in 1967.

Appendix Two

The Yeovil Railway Centre

Following the success of the steam specials to Yeovil Junction, in 1993 the South West Main Line Steam Group was formed to acquire the turntable and provide locomotive servicing facilities, the Group later becoming a company and a registered charity.

The Group originally occupied part of the former Clifton Maybank exchange sidings site to the east of the former transfer shed, and commenced to relay part of the original spur down to where it had passed under the LSWR main line.

The Yeovil Steam Festival held in October 1994 in conjunction with Network SouthEast and other organisations was the first major event with visiting steam and diesel locomotives, rail tours and the 'M7 Shuttle'. It put the Yeovil site firmly on the map.

A small 0-4-0 industrial locomotive in the form of *Pectin* arrived. Built in 1921 by Peckett of Bristol, No 1579 was delivered new to The British Aluminium Co. of Glasgow who retained her until purchased for preservation in 1971 by the 6000 Locomotive Association of Hereford. On 5th November the first brakevan rides were provided by *Pectin*, thus part of the Clifton Maybank spur returned to life and for the first time as a passenger-carrying line. Towards the end of the year class '03' 0-6-0 diesel shunter No. D2062 joined *Pectin*.

A major part of the development plan was for the erection of an engine shed to provide storage and workshop facilities for locomotives and the construction of a water tower to avoid the earlier use of water tank lorries. Planning permission for these facilities was granted by September 1996, and that year ended with the arrival on 6th December of class '20' No. 20188 (D8188).

During 1997 work commenced on construction of the engine shed and water tower, and during the October Railfair class '20' No. D8188 - fully restored - was named *River Yeo*. Work on developing the site continued apace, the completed engine shed being officially opened on 2nd October, 1999. Shortly after it was to house its first celebrity when on 13th November No. 6024 *King Edward I* was towed to Yeovil for valve gear repairs after failing whilst working a rail tour to Weymouth.

Yeovil is now the established servicing point for rail tours operating in the area, training and test runs from Eastleigh, and other movements. A diesel gala with visiting locomotives in May 2003 celebrated the tenth anniversary of the Centre. Plans for further expansion of the site raise difficulties; sandwiched between a cliff and Yeovil Junction station the future lies very much in the hands of Network Rail. In 1998 the former broad gauge transfer shed became a Grade 2 Listed Building. Until recently it had been let to a local engineering company but it has now been taken over by the Steam Centre. Much altered from its original 'open both ends' arrangement, it would not be practical to restore it to its original form. However, as the last remaining such building, and the only brick example, it is a suitable candidate for inclusion in the steam centre as a reminder that, 150 years ago, Yeovil was at the centre of the Battle of the Gauges.

The Somerset & Dorset Locomotive Co. Ltd

Since early 2001 an interesting collection of industrial locomotives has appeared in the compound of the former coal yard on the up side at Yeovil Junction which was leased from Railtrack by Yeovil Steam Centre member Mick Archer. He had purchased what had become known as the 'Shropshire Collection - an assortment of 46 diesel, 9 steam, and 1 electric locomotive, although not all have appeared on site.

On a line that never originally had a passenger service, 0-4-0 *Pectin* gives brake van rides at the Yeovil Railway Steam Centre in April 2003. Track has been re-laid along the former Clifton Maybank spur to the point where it curved and dropped under the LSWR main line behind the bushes to the left. In the foreground and to the extreme right the course of the never-laid south chord! *Author*

The intention was to set up a 'Dial- a-Loco' service for existing and fledgling preserved railways and industrial sites. On 21st March, 2002 class '20' No. 20059 arrived on site, later to be followed by No. 20177. By early in 2002 the first 0-4-0 diesel shunter had been restored and painted in Somerset & Dorset Railway blue livery. A year later, in February 2003, Peckett 0-4-0 No. 1722 of 1926 vintage had been fully restored at Tyseley. However, the company found there was not much demand for small industrial locomotives and in March 2003 it was announced that a greater part of the collection was for disposal. The company wish to concentrate on main line activities based around two class '20' diesels - Nos. 20059 *River Yeo* and 20188 - which have recently been working on Channel Tunnel Rail Link duties, with a third locomotive No. 20177 being a source of spare parts.

The locomotives of the Somerset & Dorset Locomotive Company stored in the former coal yard on the up side at Yeovil Junction in May 2003. Amongst the various shunters are class '20s' Nos. 20188 (*left*), and 20177 (*right*). *Author*

Acknowledgements

Many people have contributed to this work, ranging from answering a question to putting their knowledge and resources at my disposal, as have various organisations both large and small including: The Public Record Office, Kew; Somerset County Record Office, Taunton; Somerset County Library Service (in particular the staff at Yeovil); Dorset County Record Office, Dorchester; Dorset County Library Service (in particular the staff at Weymouth); South Somerset Museum, Yeovil; Newton Abbot Railway Studies Library; The Signalling Record Society; The Yeovil Steam Centre; The Dorset Transport Circle.

The following newspapers have been consulted: The *Western Gazette*, *Pullmans Weekly News*, *Dorset County Chronicle*, *Southern Times*, and the *Dorset Echo*.

Individuals who have given generous help include: George Pryer for the supply of track diagrams, proof reading and his professional knowledge on railway matters; Richard Sims for assistance with the broad gauge era and permission to use his diagrams of that period; R. Grimley for information concerning early bus services.

Also R. Ansell, Maureen Attwooll, S. Brown, C.L. Caddy, D. Coombes, John Day, J. Spencer Gilks, D.M. Habgood, B. Macey, J. Penny, D. Persson, D. Phillips, R.C. Riley, G.M. Stubbs, J. Sweet, B. Thirlwall.

Those who have supplied photographs are credited under their work.

Finally I would like to thank the team at Oakwood for their unfailing support, and Jean my wife for her encouragement in this project.

Railway cross-country services were always vulnerable to bus competition, typical of which was the Royal Blue service between Bournemouth and Ilfracombe, via Yeovil and Taunton. Bristol 'LL6B' No. 1269, LTA 898 with its distinctive Duple C37F body built in 1951, was one of the last half-coaches supplied to Royal Blue, However, the distinctive but dated roof luggage rack continued into the first batch of fully-fronted coaches. No. 1269 was withdrawn from service in 1963 and has been preserved.   *G.M. Stubbs*